THE BEAT GENERATION
IN NEW YORK
A WALKING TOUR OF JACK KEROUAC'S CITY

THE BEAT GENERATION IN NEW YORK

A WALKING TOUR OF JACK KEROUAC'S CITY

BY BILL MORGAN

City Lights Books
San Francisco

The Beat Generation in New York
©1997 by Bill Morgan

Cover design: Rex Ray
Book design: Nigel French & Stacey Lewis
Typography: Small World Productions
Cover photograph copyright © Allen Ginsberg Trust.
Reproduced by courtesy of Fahey/Klein Gallery, Los Angeles.

Library of Congress Cataloging–in–Publication Data

Morgan, Bill, 1949–
    The beat generation in New York: a walking tour of Jack
    Kerouac's city / Bill Morgan.
        p.   cm.
ISBN 0-87286-325-5 (pbk.)   ISBN-13: 978-0-87286-325-5
1. New York (N.Y.)—Tours.   2. Kerouac, Jack, 1922-1969—
Homes and haunts—New York (State)—New York—Guidebooks.
3. Walking—New York (State)—New York—Guidebooks.
4. Beat generation—New York (State)—New York.
I. Title.
F128 . 18 . M67 1997   97-4114
917.47' 10443—dc21   CIP

CITY LIGHTS BOOKS are edited by Lawrence Ferlinghetti and
Nancy J. Peters and published at the City Lights Bookstore,
261 Columbus Avenue, San Francisco, CA 94133.

Contents

For John Sawyer
angel friend
like Jack
both died too young

Preface

Hettie Jones

How many walls of how many dark apartments did we paint then?

And now, in how many dusty corners lurk echoes of words first imagined, quietly recited, then thrust into a world that feared and loved us, wanted in its secret heart to *be* us!

Now you can beat our New York paths with Bill Morgan, trace these eight ways to catch the sights from our lights. Here are all the familiar names, the hidden history of who lived where and what happened then, who drifted and who got evicted, who died and who survived. Here — oh wonder — is a Beat Baedeker!

You might start in the wide windy plazas at Columbia University, make the Kerouac-Ginsberg-Burroughs connection on the Upper West Side. Inhabit once more those tiny, overheated furnished rooms, stand in the middle of smoky, boozy conversations. Then take the subway to Times Square, that former hub of sleaze. Imagine Herbert Huncke in Bryant Park, conjure up ketchup soup at the Automat. Visit the Gotham Book Mart — it hasn't moved an inch since '46! — and learn from this wonderful guidebook who clerked and who was later celebrated there.

As the Beats did, you'll discover that New York is a city of neighborhoods. They can be yours! Meander through Chelsea, check out the site of Warhol's Factory, the corner that cradled the Living Theatre. Peer into the place where parties were held to staple together the latest pages of *Yugen*. Then take two tours through the Village, where boheme generations met and mingled. Have a drink at the White Horse or the Cedar (or both), coffee at the Riviera, and see for yourself, as Frank O'Hara wrote: "I was reflecting the other night meaning / I was being reflected upon that Sheridan Square / is remarkably beautiful . . ."

Too tired for more? Rest up, then hop a crosstown bus for two East Village circuits. This is where the current action is, where the wannabeats are stepping in our shoes, out front of the Dom where we danced, the Gem Spa (egg cream heaven), or at the counter of the B&H Dairy, still serving *challah* French toast after all these years. Wander farther toward the river, to Tompkins Square (East Village Central). Nearly every place you'll pass has stories, ghosts at the windows, even some living denizens at the door! Keep this book in your pocket and your eyes peeled. If you got feet, you never know who you might meet.

Introduction

One wishes that the visitor to New York City today could arrive by ship to see it: "Like all the spires and architecture and cathedrals of Europe all put together on one shelf and more massive height. You get a sense of eternity looking at Manhattan from a boat arriving — the buildings look as if they were manufacturing cosmic jazz." This was Allen Ginsberg's view sailing into the harbor in 1958.

"I roamed the streets, the bridges, Times Square, cafeterias, the waterfront, I looked up all my poet beatnik friends and roamed with them, I had love affairs with girls in the Village, I did everything with that great mad joy you get when you return to New York City." Thus spake Jack Kerouac. He tried to make the city *his* city the way that he had made Lowell, MA *his* town. But he felt he was always outside, looking in, never a part of the city. He walked on the shady side of the street, in the shadows where he felt a writer had to be. Outside, observing the action, watching, an unblinking eye.

New York City has always been a shining magnet for writers. Of course it attracted the writers of the Beat Generation. Every major writer of that movement lived in or visited New York. They all had a love-hate relationship with it. Some writers, like Michael McClure and Lew Welch, found it a brutal city that stifled creativity. Others, like Allen Ginsberg, Herbert Huncke, and Gregory Corso, found it intoxicating (if not hallucinating). Still others, like Jack Kerouac, longed to be somewhere else, yet always came back to Gotham.

Kerouac was an outlander like Thomas Wolfe. They both were lonely and homesick as they looked for successes that could only happen in New York. Kerouac fell for New York in the images created by Wolfe in his novels. "The city flashed before me like a glorious jewel, blazing with the thousand rich and brilliant facets of a life so good, so bountiful, so strangely and constantly beautiful and interesting that it seemed intolerable that I should miss a moment of it. I saw the streets swarming with the figures of great men and glorious women, and I walked among them like a conqueror, winning fiercely and exultantly by my talent, courage, and merit, the greatest tributes that the city had to offer, the highest prize of power, wealth, and fame, and the great emolument of love." "The only thing to do," Kerouac said, "is go."

The eight walking tours in this book will help you find the very places that the Beats frequented, lived, loved, and left behind. The focus is on places that are still standing. As with much of the America described in Kerouac's writing — especially in his Wolfean vision of the country in *On the Road* — it is an America fast disappearing — a post-World War II, pre-television, pre-computer America. You can still see it, if you hurry, with this book in hand.

Bill Morgan

Acknowledgments

A peripatetic walk like this could never have been put into words without a little help from our friends. Without a doubt the single most important person deserving thanks is the late Allen Ginsberg. Besides his contribution of many photographs in this book, he gave me his first-hand knowledge of places heretofore known only in his memory. Lawrence Ferlinghetti has said that Allen Ginsberg created the Beat Generation "out of whole cloth" and that without him there wouldn't have been such a beat synthesis; there would only have been separate great writers in a landscape.

Thanks also to Bob Rosenthal, Peter Hale, and Althea Crawford, patiently running the Ginsberg cottage industry. Thanks to the staff at City Lights in general and particularly Lawrence Ferlinghetti, Nancy Peters, and Stacey Lewis.

For many specific details, thanks also to: David Amram, Gordon Ball, Robert Bly, Carolyn Cassady, Helen Elliot, Robert Frank, Hettie Jones, Tim Moran, Rosebud Pettet, Simon Pettet, Rani Singh, Robert and Patricia Sutherland-Cohen, Helen Weaver, Ted Wilentz, Bob Wilson, as well as the staffs of the New York Public Library, New York University Libraries, and the Museum of the City of New York. Special thanks to John and Jim Sampas for their careful conservation of Jack Kerouac's letters and manuscripts which were so helpful in the preparation of this tour.

Final and most heartfelt thanks go to my wife, Judy. Her patience and generosity of spirit can never be repaid.

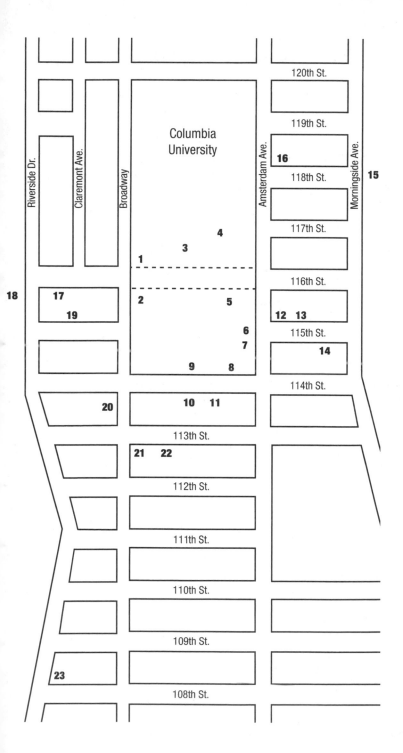

Jack Kerouac and Lucien Carr, Low Plaza Fountain, Columbia University.
©Allen Ginsberg Trust. Courtesy of Fahey/Klein Gallery, Los Angeles.

Columbia University

Length of tour: 2-2 ½ hours
Subway: 1 or 9 to 116th St./Columbia stop
Bus: M4 or M104 to 116th St.
Begin this tour on the east side of Broadway at 116th St. in front of the main gates to the Columbia campus.

Columbia College Campus

This is where the Beat Generation first appeared, like a wild seed in a city garden. The Beats first met in and around Columbia College in the 1940s and from there went on to revitalize American literature. Jack Kerouac, Allen Ginsberg, Lucien Carr, Lawrence

Ferlinghetti, and John Clellon Holmes were all students at Columbia — although they didn't all know each other at the time.

Born in Lowell, north of Boston, of French-Canadian Catholic parents, Kerouac hated the idea of going to Boston College, a Jesuit-run school, preferring instead Ivy League Columbia College. For Kerouac, Columbia served the same function as his mother's house; a place of refuge after visiting friends and partying in the heart of the city downtown. (Columbia's academic function is hardly discernible in Kerouac's writing except in *Vanity of Duluoz* and *The Town and the City.*)

There was much he liked about Horace Mann (a prep school in the Bronx where he spent a year) and Columbia, but sometimes he felt intimidated by other students' wealth and seeming sophistication. The situation did have a light side. In *Vanity of Duluoz* Kerouac wrote, "I was suddenly thrown into what amounted to an academy of incunabular Milton Berles hundreds of them wisecracking and ad-libbing on all sides, in the classroom when possible, on the field, at recess, in the subway going home into downtown Manhattan proper, over the phone at night, even years later in letters exchanged from college to college. We were all in stitches all the time."

At Columbia, Allen Ginsberg originally planned to study law to help the working-class masses as a labor lawyer. Kerouac came on a football scholarship. John Clellon Holmes attended journalism school under the G.I. Bill just after World War II. Lawrence Ferlinghetti got an M.A. in the English graduate school.

Begin the tour of the campus here at the gates to the college; Dodge Hall is the building on your left and the Journalism Building is on your right.

1   Dodge Hall, McMillin Theater

On February 5, 1959 a poetry reading by Gregory Corso, Allen Ginsberg, and Peter Orlovsky was held in McMillin Theater, now part of Dodge Hall at Broadway and 116th St. (The three had just returned from Chicago where they read in support of the editors for the censored *Chicago Review/Big Table* magazines. The press derisively covered the Beats in Chicago, treating them like "Know-Nothing Bohemians." Of course it didn't help much to have Ginsberg say "I'm crazy as a daisy" in answer to a *Time* magazine reporter's questions.)

Kerouac was scheduled to read with them at the McMillin Theater but didn't show up. The reading was staged by the English Department, the first acknowledgment of the Beats by Columbia. The students were enthusiastic but the faculty wasn't. (This wasn't the reading at which Ginsberg disrobed, revealing his poetics.) Diana Trilling, acerbic critic and wife of Ginsberg's professor Lionel Trilling, berated the Beats for their lack of manners, among other failings — "I took one look at the crowd and was certain that it would smell bad." Her lengthy review of the reading, "The Other Night at Columbia" in the Spring 1959 issue of *Partisan Review*, helped create the Beats' public image as unholy barbarians. (Much later they became "holy.")

Columbia University gates.
Photo by Bill Morgan.

2 Columbia Bookstore

In 1948 the Columbia Bookstore was located in the Journalism Building just on the south side of the entrance gates at Broadway and 116th St. In the summer of 1948, after experiencing William Blake's voice in his Harlem apartment, Allen Ginsberg visited the Columbia College bookstore. In the bookstore he had another visionary perception: He saw that everyone was wearing masks that hid their universal consciousness. These visions were a breakthrough in his perception of the universe and they had a profound influence on his life and writing. An entire book was written in 1978 by Paul Portugés about these events entitled, *The Visionary Poetics of Allen Ginsberg.*

Enter the campus through the gates at 116th St. and stop by the statue of Alma Mater. From here you can see and read about all the sites listed in No. 1-9.

3   Low Library Plaza

Left: Hal Chase, Jack Kerouac, Allen Ginsberg, and William Burroughs on Morningside Ave., ca. winter 1944.
©Allen Ginsberg Trust. Courtesy of Fahey/Klein Gallery, Los Angeles.
Right: Hal Chase and Jack Kerouac, ca. winter 1944.
©Allen Ginsberg Trust. Courtesy of Fahey/Klein Gallery, Los Angeles.

Many famous early photographs of the Beats were taken in the sunlight on the plaza of fieldstones, at the fountains in front of Low Memorial Library, and in the neighborhood.
To the right of the Low Library building is a domed chapel.

4   St. Paul's Chapel

This is one of the few original campus buildings not designed by the architectural firm of McKim, Mead, and White. In *Vanity of Duluoz* Kerouac's fictional alter-ego says:
"I'm passing St. Paul's Chapel on the campus, and going down the old wood steps they had there, here comes Mueller [David Kammerer] boundering eagerly, bearded, in the gloom, up my way, sees me, says:
   'Where's Claude? [Lucien Carr]'
   'In the West End.'
   'Thanks. I'll see ya later!'
   And I watch him rush off to his death."
   This is one of the many references in Kerouac's work to the murder of David Kammerer by Lucien Carr. Nineteen-year-old Lucien Carr was a brilliant, bold, sophisticated, and rebellious student at Columbia who was a mentor to Kerouac and Ginsberg. David Kammerer, a thirty-three-year-old former St. Louis P.E. instructor, had become obsessed with Carr's physical beauty and hounded him across the country, from Missouri to Maine to Illinois to New York. Michael Schumacher writes in his biography of Allen Ginsberg: "To people who knew [them], the situation was sad, pathetic: Lucien was decisively heterosexual, and the tall, bearded Kammerer, [was] obsessed with Lucien to the point of forsaking his life and self-respect in his hopeless pursuit . . . ." His harassment of Carr intensified until one night after everyone had

drunk far too much in the bars, Kammerer and Carr walked alone to Riverside Park, quarreling all the way. There, Kammerer made drunken threats against Celine Young, the woman Carr was living with, and then jumped Carr, telling him he loved him and demanding sex again, and threatening to kill him and take his own life. Lucien pulled out his boy scout knife and stabbed Kammerer and then weighted the body and threw it into the Hudson River.

Lucien, shaken, went to Burroughs' apartment and then to Kerouac's for advice. He and Kerouac talked it over. They drank a few beers, went to Times Square for hot dogs, watched Korda's *The Four Feathers* in a movie house, and then went to the Museum of Modern Art. Two days later, Carr turned himself in to the police. Kerouac and Burroughs were arrested for failing to report the crime; Burroughs father bailed him out, while Kerouac went to jail.

Carr was charged with second-degree murder and served time in a reformatory. Kerouac and Burroughs collaborated on a mystery novel, *And the Hippos Were Boiled in Their Tanks,* that was based on Kammerer's murder. (Fortunately for their later literary reputations, it was never published.)

The building just to the right of the Amsterdam Ave. exit from the campus is Hamilton Hall. If you walk down the steps towards Butler Library you'll see a statue of Alexander Hamilton at the entrance to the building.

5   Hamilton Hall

In March 1945, in violation of school rules, Kerouac stayed overnight in Allen Ginsberg's room here in Hamilton Hall. The next morning Dean Furey burst into the room to investigate a complaint lodged by the maid that Ginsberg had traced obscenities on his dorm window. Ginsberg had felt the maid was neglecting his room and suspected her of anti-Semitic feelings and to retaliate he'd scrawled "Fuck the Jews" and "Butler Has No Balls" in the dirt. (Nicholas Murray Butler was president of Columbia at the time.) Ginsberg was suspended. It surprised Ginsberg that the written words on the window were considered iniquitous by the authorities; he had assumed they'd be enraged by his having an illegal guest. It was the first of his encounters with censorship of "dangerous" words.

Kerouac liked professors Mark Van Doren and Raymond Weaver who shared an office at 306 Hamilton. He took Mark Van Doren's Shakespeare course and got an A. He flunked chemistry. He set a record for cutting classes and stayed in his dorm room to write and read. Mark Van Doren taught at Columbia from 1920 until 1959, and among his students were Allen Ginsberg, Thomas

Merton, Lionel Trilling, Louis Zukofsky, and Lawrence
Ferlinghetti. (Raymond Weaver was the Herman Melville scholar
who discovered the manuscript of *Billy Budd* in an old trunk.)

Next to Van Doren and Weaver in 305 Hamilton was Lionel
Trilling's office, and Ginsberg was one of his students. Trilling, one
of the country's most incisive literary critics and on the *Partisan
Review* and *Kenyon Review,* lived nearby at 620 W. 116th St.,
where Ginsberg was a frequent visitor and looked to him for advice and encouragement. On several occasions Trilling and Van
Doren helped Ginsberg out of scrapes with the college adminis-
tration. Twenty years later, when Ginsberg returned to read at Columbia as a famous poet, he dedicated the reading to Trilling.
The building to the right of Hamilton Hall is Hartley Hall.

Hamilton Hall (left) and Hartley Hall (right).
Photo by Bill Morgan.

6   Hartley Hall

Kerouac first moved into a room in Hartley Hall in the fall of 1940 after his preparatory year at Horace Mann. In *Vanity of Duluoz* he wrote,
"Here we stood in this sort of drear room overlooking Amsterdam
Avenue, a wooden desk, bed, chairs, bare walls, and one huge cock-
roach suddenly rushing off. Furthermore in walks a little kid with
glasses wearing a blue skullcap and announces he will be my room-
mate for the year and that he is a pledge with the Wi Delta Woowoo
fraternity and that's the skullcap." Allen Ginsberg, Langston Hughes,
and Herbert Gold also lived in Hartley Hall at various times. (Herbert
Gold, later a permanent resident of San Francisco, knew Ginsberg but
was never very close to the Beat group.)
Just to the right of Hartley Hall was Livingston Hall.

7   Livingston Hall

As soon as he could, in the fall of 1940, Kerouac transferred from his "drear room" at Hartley to Livingston Hall. From his new room, he could see Butler Library and the Lion's Den. In *Vanity of Duluoz* Kerouac writes: "there were no cockroaches and where b'God I had a room all to myself, on the second floor, overlooking the beautiful trees and walkways of the campus and overlooking, to my greatest delight, besides the Van Am Quadrangle, the library itself, the new one, with its stone frieze running around entire with the names engraved in stone forever: 'Goethe . . . Voltaire . . . Shakespeare . . . Molière . . . Dante.'"

Hal Chase, who introduced Neal Cassady to the Columbia group, also lived in Livingston, as did poet John Giorno more than ten years later, in 1956. (The building is now called Wallach Hall.) *The corner building is John Jay Hall.*

8   John Jay Hall

Kerouac's football coach, Louis Little, had an office at 401 John Jay, as did the head of Freshman football, Coach Furey. This was the same Dean Furey who caught Kerouac sleeping overnight in Ginsberg's dorm room. The training table for the football team, and the dining hall for the entire college, was in John Jay. (Here evidently Kerouac favored suppers of milk, meat, and dry toast.)

During the 1940 Army football game, Kerouac broke his leg. Once it healed, he had to work here as a waiter to pay for his food allowance. (Years later he remembered refilling Thomas Mann's coffee cup.)

The Lion's Den was on the lower level of John Jay Hall. The social center of the campus in the 1940s, it was a grill room with space large enough for dancing. Kerouac loved the Lion's Den, where as a football player he could have steaks and hot fudge sundaes whenever he wanted.

[Note: Baker Football Field. Although a hundred blocks farther north on Broadway at 215th St., Baker Field is a part of the Columbia campus. Kerouac practiced football here. "At dusk you could see the lights of New York across the Harlem River, it was right smack in the middle of New York City, even tugboats went by in the Harlem River, a great bridge crossed it full of cars, I couldn't understand what had gone wrong." He had disagreements with head coach Lou Little, and was used sparingly on the championship football team. Kerouac and his father, Leo, were not shy in voicing their opinion that Jack should play more, and this no doubt added to the problem. The stadium has been renovated since those glory days, but the field still has a 1940s feeling. To

visit Baker Field, take the #1 subway from 116th St. to 215th St.
(Allow 1 ½ hours for the round trip.)
*The large building just to the right of John Jay is Butler
Library.*

9   Butler Library
In 1934 the Low Library was replaced with this building, named
for Columbia President, Nicholas Murray Butler. Lawrence
Ferlinghetti spent most of his time at Columbia in this library, re-
searching his 1948 Master's thesis "Ruskin's Turner: Child of
Light." He literally spent months pouring over the beautiful letter-
press Kelmscott editions of Ruskin's *Stones of Venice* and *Modern
Painters* with their full-color lithographs of W.J. Turner's works.
Ginsberg and Kerouac could sometimes be found here, pursuing
their own interests, academic and otherwise.
*Exit the campus through the gate just to the right of the Butler
Library. If the gate is closed walk around to the corner of
Broadway and 114th St., turn left onto 114th St., and stop in
front of 538 W. 114th St.*

10   Phi Gamma Delta Fraternity
On the south side of W. 114th St. is a row of college fraternity
houses. For a very short while in 1940 Jack Kerouac was a pledge
at the Phi Gamma Delta fraternity at 538 W. 114th St. He described it in *Vanity of Duluoz,* "where I was a 'pledge' but refused
to wear the little blue skullcap, in fact told them to shove it and in-
sisted instead on giving me the beer barrel which was almost
empty, and raised it above my head at dawn and drained it of its
dregs." In an arc above the door of this four-story yellow brick
house, are the Greek letters ΦΓΔ.
Just next door is No. 536 W. 114th St.

11   Allen Ginsberg
Early in 1948, Allen Ginsberg took a tiny room (#3C) at 536 W.
114th St. near the Columbia campus, now the ΠΚΑ fraternity.
Here in this small, four-story yellow brick building, he assembled
the poems called "Denver Doldrums," written while in Denver
with Neal Cassady. Ginsberg's brother Eugene Brooks, then a
young lawyer just out of NYU, took the room when Ginsberg left
in 1949.
*Walk east on 114th St. to the next corner with Amsterdam Ave.,
turn left one block, and then right onto 115th St. Stop in front
of No. 419.*

12   Joan Vollmer Adams

The large yellow brick
Cragsmoor Apartments at 419
W. 115th St. was the second and
last of the Morningside Heights
"pads" of the nascent Beats.
Around Christmas 1944, the
newly married Edie and Jack
Kerouac returned from Michigan and moved into apartment
51 with Joan Vollmer Adams.
Joan had her infant daughter,
Julie, with her. Suspended from
Columbia for a year after the
dorm window graffiti episode,
Ginsberg moved into Joan's
apartment in March 1945 to share a room with Hal Chase, an an-
thropology student from Denver. In the fall of 1945, a seminal dis-
cussion later known as "The Night of the Wolfeans" took place
here. Kerouac and Chase took the side of Thomas Wolfe; Ginsberg
and Burroughs were the non-Wolfeans. In January 1946,
Burroughs moved into the apartment and remained until April
when he was arrested for forging a doctor's prescription for nar-
cotics. In June he received a four-month suspended sentence and
was remanded to St. Louis and his parents' custody. In the summer of 1946, life around the apartment fell apart. (Burroughs was
off to St. Louis, Ginsberg to sea, Kerouac to his mother's, and
Adams herself suffered from amphetamine-induced delusions.)
In October 1946 Adams was hospitalized in Bellevue's psychiatric
ward. Burroughs bailed her out in December 1946, and they became common-law companions for the rest of her life. She died in
1951 in Mexico City when Burroughs tried to shoot a glass off the
top of her head, à la William Tell. In *Vanity of Duluoz*, Kerouac
called the time in this apartment "a year of evil decadence."

Joan Adams, ca. winter 1944.
©Allen Ginsberg Trust. Courtesy of
Fahey/Klein Gallery, Los Angeles.

13   W. 115th St. from Amsterdam to Morningside

Walking down 115th St. between Amsterdam and Morningside,
Allen Ginsberg wrote in his journal, "Looking down on the street,
I was struck by the fact that it was a stage—really, truly a stage. I
played my part on it—I walked the street, lonely, in love, recover-
ing from love. I had a tragic role. Yet I was conscious of my role, so
conscious, in fact, that I almost treasured it for its nobility. Now I
am acting this tragedy. In years to come I shall walk down this
street, this stage, and look at it in retrospect. It shall not then be a

part of the present, but a reminder of the past to me. I shall value
it and love it for what it once meant."
Walk farther east on 115th St. to the south side of the street in
front of the parking lot where No. 404 used to be.

14   Warren Hall

The blood of poet Kerouac.
©1995 The Estate of Jack and Stella Kerouac. Permission granted by the
executor John Sampas.

In the winter of 1943-1944, Kerouac found a job as switchboard
operator at the Warren Hall Residence Club at 404 W. 115th St. The
building has been torn down and the space is now a parking lot.

In July 1944, Allen Ginsberg moved into Room 6Q of Warren
Hall. The rooms were clean and cheap at $8 per week. Lucien Carr
lived on the same floor in room 6V; David Kammerer sometimes
climbed in the window from the fire escape to watch Carr sleep. In
Vanity of Duluoz, Kerouac changed the name to Dalton Hall; elsewhere he called it the Hotel Bates.

In late 1944 after jumping ship in the Merchant Marine,
Kerouac took a room on the sixth floor in Warren Hall, where he
really began his life as a writer. Lucien Carr's girlfriend, Celine,
visited Kerouac here when Carr was sent to prison, and Kerouac
tried in vain to sleep with her, taking her flirtations seriously. He
used his own blood to write "The Blood of the Poet" on a card that
he hung on the wall. Around Christmas 1944, Kerouac's wife Edie
came to live with him in Warren Hall. Shortly afterwards they
moved to 118th St.
Walk to the corner of Morningside Ave., turn left, and stop at
the entrance to the park at 118th St.

15 Morningside Park

This park divides Morningside Heights from Harlem. The entrance is at W. 118th St. and Morningside Ave. After killing Kammerer and going to the Village to talk with Burroughs, Lucien Carr came back to Joan Vollmer Adams' apartment on W. 118th St. to see Kerouac.

Entrance to Morningside Park.
Photo by Bill Morgan.

They decided that Carr should get rid of the knife and Kammerer's eyeglasses in Morningside Park. They went into the park at 118th St. and down the stone steps. To distract anyone who might be looking, Kerouac pretended to urinate while Carr buried the eyeglasses, and then they dropped the knife down a storm drain in Harlem. (For taking part in this, Kerouac was held as a material witness.)

Walk west on 118th St. almost to the corner of Amsterdam and stop at No. 421.

16 Joan Adams and Edie Parker

At 421 W. 118th St. is a six-floor yellow brick apartment building. Kerouac often said that the happiest days of his life were spent in a four-bedroom apartment in the rear of this building. He described it in *The Town and the City* as being "near the wild Spanish neighborhoods, yet within a short distance of the Irish tenements and saloons of Amsterdam, the blazing kosher-marts, ho-

421 W. 118th St.
Photo by Bill Morgan.

tels and movie theaters of Upper Broadway, and the sleek towers of Central Park West." Here Kerouac and Edie Kerouac Parker would have their favorite snack of cold asparagus with mayonnaise and ripe olives. It was a time when he was still optimistic about the fortune and fame yet to come.

While Joan Adams' husband was away in the service, she filed for divorce. In the meantime, her sixteen-year-old Columbia student lover, John Kingsland, lived here. Not liking the fact that their son was living with an older, married woman, his parents interceded. Kingsland moved out. Short of money, Joan and Edie took in boarders, one of them Hal Chase, a graduate student from Denver, through whom they met Neal Cassady.

Between October 1943 and 1944 apartment 62 was an unofficial hang-out for the Beats. Lucien Carr brought William Burroughs up to the sixth floor to meet Kerouac in February 1944. Burroughs wanted to know how to join the Merchant Marine but never followed the advice Kerouac gave him. Allen Ginsberg also first met Kerouac here, although it was hardly a meeting of "kindred spirits." They both remembered a shy Ginsberg saying when they were introduced, "Discretion is the better part of valor"; before long, however, they became very close. Edie Kerouac Parker recalled, "When the apartment got noisy or there was a lot going on, they [Kerouac and Ginsberg] would go to the Columbia music library and be there for hours, listening to the same record with earphones in the same booth—Allen half asleep, Jack reading."

The morning after killing David Kammerer, Lucien Carr came here to tell Kerouac. After Carr confessed, Kerouac was arrested by the police here. While he was in jail, Jack married Edie Parker (the police acting as witnesses) in a City Hall ceremony on August 22, 1944. Thus they were able to get bail money from her wealthy family. Kerouac's own father wanted nothing to do with his son-gone-bad. (Ten years later, in 1956, in the apartment building next door at 423 W. 118th St., Joyce Glassman Johnson [author of *Minor Characters*] found a room, just before she met Kerouac.)
Turn left onto Amsterdam Ave. and cut back across the Columbia campus at 116th St. Walk straight across 116th St., down the hill to No. 620, almost at the end of the street.

17   Joyce Glassman Johnson

Just off the Columbia campus near the corner of Riverside Dr. at 620 W. 116th St. is the large old apartment building in which Joyce Johnson was raised, and where Lionel Trilling also lived. It's possible that she might have run into Kerouac or Ginsberg on one of their visits to Trilling's home. Ten years later she would be dating Kerouac, and thirty years later she would write about this period of her life in *Minor Characters*.

Hettie Jones lived in the same building from October 1955 through December 1956, when she was doing graduate study at Columbia and working for the Center for Mass Communication of Columbia University Press.
Continue to the corner and stop at the entrance to Riverside Park.

18   Riverside Park

Entrance to Riverside Park.
Photo by Bill Morgan.

On the night of August 14, 1944 Lucien Carr killed David Kammerer here, just over the hill from W. 116th St. After the murder, the *Daily News* ran a photograph of Carr looking at the murder site from this location.

Many times Carr and Kerouac had sat on the grass here watching the freighters going to sea. Carr had thought of going to France to escape Kammerer's aggressive sexual advances.
Walk one block south on Riverside Dr. and then turn left onto 115th St. About midway up the block stop in front of No. 627.

19   Allen Ginsberg

In October 1944, Allen Ginsberg moved into an old fraternity house at 627 W. 115th St. that had been turned into a dorm during the war. While living here Ginsberg was classified 4F by the Selective Service draft board for admitting that he had homosexual tendencies. In those days such a confession barred a person from military service.
Continue up 115th St. and turn right onto Broadway. Stop in front of the West End Bar at No. 2911 Broadway between 113th St. and 114th St.

20   West End Bar

Allen Ginsberg wrote in his journal (1944) that "The West End was a university replica of a Greenwich Village dive. The café was divided by a partition into two sides; in the evenings, Otto, the chef, presided over the lunch room half. Otto was a nasty tempered and sharped tongued Dane who resented taking orders. Since he was a counterman he found much to resent. On the other side of the partition was a long, well attended bar. There was a cigarette machine as one entered the revolving door, a jukebox, and a men's room at the far end. Bill or Johnny usually tended the bar. Johnny was an Irish Catholic, a great shouldered man with a large nose and a strong sense of morals. He thought that all students were communists."

West End Bar.
Photo by Bill Morgan.

Ginsberg first met Neal Cassady and his wife LuAnne at the West End, just after their arrival in New York City in 1946. Cassady described Ginsberg in his autobiography *The First Third*. Most of the New York characters whom Jack Kerouac used in *The Town and the City* were regulars here: Ginsberg, Lucien Carr and his girlfriend Celine Young, David Kammerer, and Allan Temko (later an architectural critic on *The San Francisco Chronicle*). One night Kerouac, defending Celine Young, got into a fight with two sailors, and Johnny the bartender had to break it up. Another night Carr rolled Kerouac down the street in a barrel.

Diana Trilling stigmatized the bar in a *Partisan Review* piece as "that dim waystation of undergraduate debauchery on Morningside Heights."

Today no debauchery is to be found. It is now a bright and open restaurant and bar, more than double the size of the original, with huge windows. About the only thing that might be the same is the old tile floor, hollowly echoing with the footsteps of generations.
Go south on Broadway and stop at the corner of 113th St.

21   Yorkshire Residence Club
The Yorkshire Residence Club stood in the large eight-story yellow brick building at the corner of Broadway and W. 113th St. It is now Columbia's McBain Hall with the entrance on the side street at 562 W. 113th St. "In the Yorkshire were a group of presumably simpatico young intellectuals with a generally socialist and psy-

chological orientation," wrote Carl Solomon of the residence hotel where he lived just before being sent to Pilgrim State Hospital. Allen Ginsberg addressed his "Howl" to Solomon while he was in Pilgrim State (in the poem he calls it Rockland).

Walk east past the Yorkshire on 113th St. and stop in front of No. 554.

22   Joyce Glassman Johnson

Joyce Glassman Johnson lived in what she called a "dark and cavernous" apartment on the first floor just up the stairs of the brownstone at 554 W. 113th St. She moved in during 1957, and Kerouac lived with her here during the first days after the publication of *On the Road* that fall. He renamed her cat Ti Gris after a cat he had in Lowell. Kerouac considered Johnson the one person he could have been happy with, but even here he set up his own private room in the back where he slept with the window open during the coldest weather, alone. Kerouac described his life at this time in *Desolation Angels.*

554 W. 113th St.
Photo by Bill Morgan.

Return to Broadway and turn left. Walk south on Broadway several blocks and turn right onto W. 108th St. Follow it almost to the corner of Riverside Dr. and stop at the doorway marked 360 Riverside Dr. even though you're on W.108th.

23   William Burroughs

William Burroughs existed in the Rutherfurd Apartments at 360 Riverside Dr. in December 1944, before moving in to Joan Adams' apartment on W. 115th St. He had just returned from St. Louis, where he had retreated after the Kammerer murder. Ginsberg and Kerouac visited here many times, and Burroughs began lending them books by Cocteau, Kafka, Blake, Hart Crane, and other subversives and visionaries. Burroughs began a program of amateur psychoanalysis with Ginsberg and Kerouac for an hour a day.

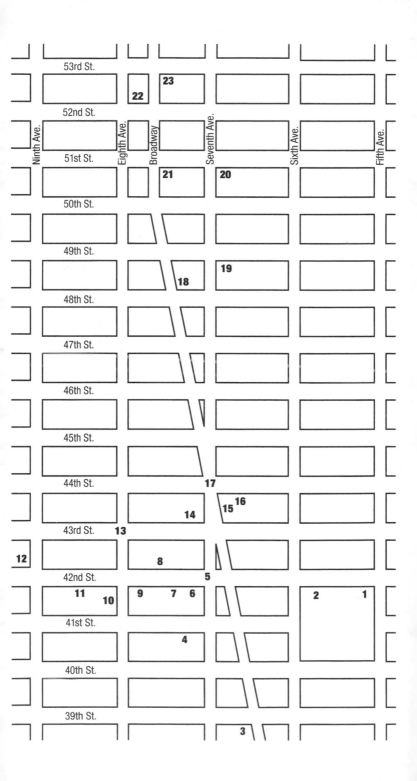

William Burroughs, 1953.
©Allen Ginsberg Trust. Courtesy of Fahey/Klein Gallery, Los Angeles.

Times Square

Length of tour: 2-2 ½ hours
Subway: B, D, F or Q to 42nd St. or 7 to Fifth Ave.
Bus: M1, 2, 3, 4, 5, 6, 7, 18, 42, 104, Q32 to Fifth Ave. and 42nd St.
Begin this tour at the New York Public Library on Fifth Ave. at 42nd St.

1　New York Public Library

The main research branch of the New York Public Library is essential to students of the Beat Generation. It has one of the best public collections in the world of books and manuscripts by Jack Kerouac, Allen Ginsberg, and Peter Orlovsky. You can find Orlovsky's journals and an early draft of Ginsberg's "Howl" here, as well as manuscripts by William Burroughs, Gregory Corso, and many others associated with the Beats. In the Berg Collection on the third floor are the original notebooks and manuscripts for Kerouac's *Maggie Cassidy, Mexico City Blues, Book of Dreams, Some of the Dharma,* and *Satori in Paris,* to name some of the highlights.

Kerouac said if he ever lived near this library he would write a "Civil War novel which I want to parallel Tolstoy's 1812 hangups in 1850's." In 1953 Allen Ginsberg spent weeks studying Chinese paintings in the Fine Arts Room. Carl Solomon read the Lettrist magazine, *La Dictature Lettriste,* here and discovered books by Isidore Issou and French Lettrists. As a boy, Gregory Corso wrote his very first poem, "Sea Chanty," here. Julian Beck of the Living Theatre worked here as a typist in 1952-1953. His wife, Judith Malina, wrote in her journals of looking for plays by Apollinaire and Yeats: "At closing time the readers move through the halls into elevators, like sleepwalkers."

Go west 1/2 block on 42nd St. and stop in the park directly behind the library.

2 Bryant Park

This is one of the few green spaces in midtown Manhattan and it is always crowded on a sunny day. Originally it was a potter's field, and the poor were buried here through the early 1800s. Later, a reservoir was built where the library is today, and this park was created. In the 1970s the park became a hang-out for drug dealers. In the late 1980s it was closed for several years during construction of an underground storage area for the library. The park has been reopened and you will discover statues of Gertrude Stein and Johann Goethe, a curious couple to be found together.

Herbert Huncke was hustling here in the 1940s and 1950s. In an early draft of "Howl," Allen Ginsberg refers to Huncke: "who wandered in bryant park digging the color of the negro of the evening sky . . ." On one occasion, Huncke and a friend were trying to break into a car to steal suitcases and overcoats for drug money. They couldn't get the door open so they pulled up a "Keep Off the Grass" sign and used it to break the car windows. They were caught and Huncke was sent to Riker's Island for six months, his first time in prison, but not his last.

Poet Paul Blackburn also made use of the "Keep Off" signs in Bryant Park in his poem "Bryant Park."

Walk to Sixth Ave., turn south one block to 41st St., and turn right one block west on 41st St. to the corner of Broadway. Here you can read the description of the old Metropolitan Opera House which no longer exists.

3 Metropolitan Opera

Before Lincoln Center was built, the Metropolitan Opera House was at Broadway and 39th St. One night in the mid-1940s, Lucien Carr, Allen Ginsberg, Celine Young, and Edie Parker went to the opera. In *Vanity of Duluoz* Kerouac describes how Carr created a commotion in the balcony, and when the ushers came to eject them they all ran backstage and underground through a labyrinth of hallways and rooms and made their escape onto Seventh Ave. *Return to 41st St. and walk the very short block left to Seventh Ave. Just past this corner on the south side of W. 41st St. is the Nederland Theater.*

4 National Theatre

The Nederland Theater at 208 W. 41st St. was called the National Theatre for a short period in the 1940s. On January 7, 1948, Kerouac took a break from his work on *The Town and the City* for a matinee performance of *Crime and Punishment.* The play, adapted from Dostoyevsky's novel, starred John Gielgud and Lillian Gish. Kerouac went by himself to watch this drama of a young man racked by guilt over a crime he'd committed.
Go one block north on Seventh Ave. to the corner of 42nd St.

5 IRT Subway/Times Square Area

Herbert Huncke, Times Square area hotel, 1953.
©Allen Ginsberg Trust. Courtesy of Fahey/Klein Gallery, Los Angeles.

The IRT subway train (the entrance is on this corner) is where Leon Levinsky (Ginsberg) played Peeping Tom in Kerouac's novel *The Town and the City.* In the story Leon cut a hole in a newspaper through which he peered at other riders to see how they'd react.

He finds that only a four-year-old boy isn't afraid of him. Kerouac wrote, "...they [children] haven't had time to burden themselves with character structure and personality armors and systems of moral prejudice and God knows what. Therefore they're free to live and laugh, and free to love."

Times Square technically begins one block north of the corner where Broadway intersects Seventh Ave. Read this description before continuing across 42nd St.

For a century, Times Square has been the hub of New York City. It's been a powerful magnet for all kinds of people looking for all kinds of action, including the Beats. John Clellon Holmes in his novel *Go* describes "the glaring nighttime confusion of Times Square, its unruly bars, teeming cafeterias and all-night movies." In the 1940s and 1950s it was the center of nightlife: bars, theater, movies, all-night cafeterias, Pokerino arcades, quick-change artists, conmen, and hustlers of every variety. Kerouac described arriving at Times Square after a cross-country trip, "right in the middle of a rush hour, too, seeing with my innocent road-eyes the absolute madness and fantastic hoorair of New York with its millions and millions hustling forever for a buck among themselves, the mad dream—grabbing, taking, giving, sighing, dying, just so they could be buried in those awful cemetery cities beyond Long Island City."

Herbert Huncke arrived in New York from Chicago around 1940. He quickly became part of the Times Square hustling scene. When Ginsberg, Burroughs, Kerouac, and others from Columbia arrived, he was their guide, a veritable Virgil through that modern Inferno.

In May of 1941 Kerouac and his father went to see a French-language movie on Times Square. After the movie they ran into a classmate of Kerouac who told him that he'd been elected vice-president of the Columbia sophomore class. "My father immediately took my picture in a ratty Times Square booth," he proudly wrote in *Vanity of Duluoz*. Everything on the Square interested Kerouac. He writes in *Lonesome Traveler*, "Emerging from the Seventh Avenue subway on 42nd Street, you pass the john, which is the beatest john in New York," and you learn more than you want to know about it.

In *The Town and the City*, Kerouac described the bus ride into New York City and through Times Square as vividly as anyone ever has. The signs were "a blazing daytime in themselves, a magical universe of lights sparkling and throbbing with the intensity of a flash explosion." He describes the "soldiers, sailors, the panhandlers and drifters, the zoot-suiters, the hoodlums, the young

men who washed dishes in cafeterias . . . the hitch-hikers, the
hustlers, the drunks, the battered lonely young Negroes, the twin-
kling little Chinese, the dark Puerto Ricans, and the varieties of
dungareed young Americans in leather jackets who were seamen
and mechanics and garagemen." And just as he was digging everyone and everything, he runs into Allen Ginsberg, Herbert
Huncke, and Jack Melody walking up the street looking for the action. In *Lonesome Traveler* Kerouac quotes Gregory Corso's poem
"Power": "Standing on a street corner waiting for no one is Power."

The founders of the Living Theatre, Judith Malina and Julian
Beck, went to Loew's Movie Theater on 42nd St. on their first date
in September 1943. They saw Joan Crawford in *Above Suspicion.*
Thus did their life in the theater begin.
Walk west on 42nd St. towards Eighth Ave. and stop at No. 210.

6   Chase's Cafeteria

Just to the left of the New Amsterdam Theater marquee stood
Chase's Cafeteria at 210 W. 42nd St. It was a hangout for hoodlums
when Kerouac, Allen Ginsberg, Neal Cassady, and Herbert Huncke
went there. In *On the Road* Kerouac called it Ritzy's Bar. He wrote,
"you don't see a single girl, even in the booths, just a great mob of
young men dressed in all varieties of hoodlum cloth, from red
shirts to zoot suits."

In 1945 Professor Alfred Kinsey canvassed people in this bar for
his pioneering study of American sexual practices. Ginsberg writes:
"I first met Herbert Huncke when William S. Burroughs was explor-
ing the lumpen world of Eighth Avenue and 42nd Street in 1945. I
think Burroughs had some syrettes of morphine, and Huncke
bought them from him. At that time Huncke was a scout for Dr.
Alfred Kinsey, who was interested in the floating population around
Times Square — the thieves, junkies, sportsmen, gamblers, racing
touts — so Huncke made appointments for myself and Burroughs
and Jack Kerouac to be debriefed by Dr. Kinsey. My own statistics
were somewhat virginal at the time and were integrated into
Kinsey's *Sexual Behavior of the Human Male.*"
On the same side of the street stop next door at No. 220.

7   Grant's Cafeteria

Grant's Cafeteria at 220 W. 42nd St. stood between the New
Amsterdam Theater and the Harris Theatre in the Candler building, named for Coca-Cola magnate, Asa Candler.

Grant's was Jack Kerouac's favorite place to chow down on
Times Square. In *Lonesome Traveler* he described the menu and
the regulars. He wasn't rushed and could hang out for hours over a

cup of coffee. In his novel, *Go,* John Clellon Holmes wrote, "the huge, teeming cafeteria on the corner of Broadway, where even steam tables fouled the air with a wild conflict of smells and servers, presiding over them like unshaven wizards, imprecated the shuffling crowds indifferently while greasy, beardless busboys, like somnambulists, moved among the littered tables mechanically." Holmes included Kerouac in his cafeteria scene.

On the north side of the street is No. 225.

8   Bickford's Cafeteria

Site of Bickford's Cafeteria, 225 W. 42nd St.
Photo by Bill Morgan.

In the middle of the block on the north side of W. 42nd St. at No. 225 was Bickford's Cafeteria. In *Lonesome Traveler* Kerouac described Bickford's as the greatest stage on Times Square. It was right under the Apollo Theatre marquee (not to be confused with the more famous Apollo Theater on 125th St. in Harlem). Herbert Huncke, Vicki Russell, Allen Ginsberg, Jack Kerouac, Jack Melody, John Clellon Holmes, William S. Burroughs, Lucien Carr, and David Kammerer hung out here at one time or another. People practically lived here and Kerouac said Huncke could spend eighteen hours a day sitting at a window. Kerouac sat at a table in Bickford's one day and wrote the story called "Confession of Three Murders."

Ginsberg worked here briefly bussing tables and mopping floors. When he wrote "Howl" a few years later he included the line, "who sank all night in submarine light of Bickford's floated out and sat through the stale beer afternoon in desolate Fugazzi's, listening to the crack of doom on the hydrogen jukebox."

And William Burroughs wrote, "not only did they have very good food, excellent food and very cheap, but also they were all meeting places, drug meeting places, you had to be careful that the manager didn't spot it. But all the cafeterias were meets. The 42nd St.

Bickford's was a notorious hang-out for thieves and pimps and whores and fags and dope pushers and buyers and everything."
On the south side of 42nd St. look at No. 250.

9   Horn & Hardart Automat

Now just a memory to many New Yorkers, the Horn & Hardart Automats were cafeterias with dishes of food behind little windows which you opened with a coin. They were the cheapest places to eat in the city. A very poor writer could go there, buy a cup of tea with some bread and make pickle relish sandwiches, or get refills of hot water and make tomato soup out of ketchup. The Automats offered such things as macaroni and cheese or baked beans with bacon for a nickel. They were open all night which made them a favorite of the Times Square hustlers. Bill Garver supported his drug habit by stealing overcoats and then pawning them for a few dollars. According to Burroughs, Garver was one of the few junkies who took pleasure in seeing non-users develop a dope habit. Sometimes he provided free drugs to develop regular customers. Ginsberg remembers Garver sharing drugs with him, but he was careful not to get hooked. (He had greater things to develop.) The Horn & Hardart that stood here at 250 W. 42nd St. was long ago replaced by peepshow arcades. There was another popular automat at 1447 Broadway near 41st St. and many branches throughout the city. The last automat closed in 1991 at the corner of 42nd St. and Third Ave., and with it died a whole American subculture. Europe had its cafés, America had its cafeterias, and many a literary work came out of them.
At the corner of Eighth Ave. and 42nd St. you'll see a large bus station.

10   Port Authority Bus Terminal

Carl Solomon worked at the bookstore in the Port Authority Bus Terminal in the 1970s. The job gave him the opportunity to read and develop his own weird sensibility. He had another job as a messenger in the Midtown area and wrote about it in his book *Emergency Messages.* (City Lights Books later published Solomon's *Mishaps Perhaps* and *More Mishaps,* leading one critic to speculate that everything he wrote was a mishap.)
Continue west on 42nd St. to the middle of the next block to a large green building at No. 330.

11   McGraw-Hill Building

The McGraw-Hill Building at 330 W. 42nd St. was built in 1931. Kerouac describes it in *Lonesome Traveler* as "the green McGraw-Hill building gaping up in the sky, higher than you'd believe — lonely all by itself down towards the Hudson River where freighters wait in the rain for their Montevideo limestone." McGraw-Hill published *Lonesome Traveler* in 1960 and, after Kerouac's death, his *Visions of Cody*. Ginsberg describes the building in "Back on Times Square, Dreaming of Times Square" as "the green & grooking McGraw Hill offices."

McGraw-Hill building.
Photo by Bill Morgan.

Beyond McGraw-Hill on the south side of 42nd St. is the entrance to the Lincoln Tunnel. Kerouac's and Cassady's cross-country trips started at this tunnel as did the trips of millions — a veritable gateway to America. Turn right onto Ninth Ave. and walk half a block north. On the west side of the street in the middle of the block look for where No. 596 Ninth Ave. would have stood.

12   Seven Arts Coffee Gallery

On the block bounded by Ninth Ave., 42nd St., Tenth Ave., and 43rd St. stands two forty-five-story apartment buildings known as Manhattan Plaza. The Seven Arts Coffee Gallery was located at 596 Ninth Ave. between 42nd and 43rd St. It is mentioned by Kerouac in *Lonesome Traveler*. Seven Arts flourished for only a year and a half but it attracted many writers of the Beat Generation. In a second floor storefront John Rapinic organized poetry readings that became regular events in 1959. Although far from the literary scene downtown, it somehow became an important venue for poets like Ray

Bremser, Gregory Corso, Diane di Prima, Ginsberg, LeRoi Jones, Kerouac, and Peter Orlovsky.

Left: Gregory Corso and Ray Bremser, 1959.
Photo by Giorgina Reid. Courtesy Allen Ginsberg Trust.
Right: LeRoi Jones and Allen Ginsberg, 1959.
Courtesy Allen Ginsberg Trust.

Turn right again onto 43rd St., walk one block east, and stop at the corner of Eighth Ave.

13 Angler Bar

A haunt of the Beats in the mid-1940s was the Angler Bar (also called The Angle in many books) near the corner of Eighth Ave. and 43rd St. For a time, William Burroughs, Edie Parker, Jack Kerouac, Joan Adams, Allen Ginsberg, and Herbert Huncke came here almost every day. Burroughs wrote of it in *Junky*, "This bar was a meeting place for 42nd Street hustlers, a peculiar breed of four-flushing, would-be criminals." Later in *Junky*, Subway Mike is stabbed by Whitey in this bar. Shortly after 1945 the name of the bar was changed to the Roxy Grill, no doubt catering to different kinds of anglers.

In the Angler Herbert Huncke told stories about people he had known that were later collected into *Huncke's Journal*. Kerouac wrote in *Vanity of Duluoz* that "we hung out in the vile bar on Eighth Avenue around the corner from 42nd Street." This is where Huncke arranged for Burroughs, Joan Adams, and Ginsberg to meet Dr. Kinsey for interviews for his report on American sexual practices. Huncke earned $2 for each referral.

Continue walking east on 43rd St. to the northwest corner of Seventh Ave. and 43rd St.

14 The Paramount

The Paramount Theater, opened at 1501 Broadway in 1926, was a cavernous stage built for live entertainment as well as film. The building is still here, but only the small Paramount Cafe uses the name. Kerouac came here often. He may have come here for the first time in the fall of 1939, when he played hooky on his second day of school at Horace Mann. He went to the Apollo Movie Theatre on 42nd St. for a double feature, and then on to the Paramount to watch "probably Alice Fay in the rain with a spaghetti signboard because she failed to pay her restaurant bill" *(Vanity of Duluoz)*.

Later that year he returned to the Paramount to interview Glenn Miller backstage for the Horace Mann school newspaper. Almost 30 years later when he wrote about the interview, the thing that vividly stuck in his mind was hearing Miller use the awful word "shit."

On April 17, 1952, Allen Ginsberg and his brother Eugene Brooks saw the epic *Quo Vadis* here. The Paramount had the largest marquee that Ginsberg had ever seen. The theater closed in 1965, after spawning baby Paramounts all over America.
Walk north one block to W. 44th St. and stop on the corner.

15 Hector's Cafeteria

Hector's was a popular chain of Jewish cafeterias in the city. The Times Square branch was at 1506 Broadway on the east side between 43rd and 44th Streets, long ago torn down and replaced with twin cineplex movies. In *Visions of Cody* Kerouac described Hector's: "A glittering counter — decorative walls — but nobody notices noble old ceiling of ancient decorated in fact almost baroque (Louis XV?) plaster

Neal Cassady, photo booth portrait.
©Allen Ginsberg Trust. Courtesy of Fahey/ Klein Gallery, Los Angeles.

now browned a smoky rich tan color . . . " In 1946 this was the first glimpse of New York Neal Cassady had when he arrived from Denver with his wife, LuAnne. Cassady had been expecting a typical Denver-style cafeteria, but he found this enormous ornate place and immediately fell for the decadent driving energy of Times Square.
Turn right on 44th St. and stop at No. 142.

16 Dazian's Theatrical Fabric House

Carolyn Robinson (Cassady) lived in New York for a brief period before she met Neal Cassady. As a Bennington College student she came to the city in the spring of 1943 to work in the theater costume industry, first as a saleswoman and later as a designer. The

job at Dazian's, in this white stone and brick building at 142 W. 44th St., earned her college credits toward a degree in Drama. And she had a marvelous time while living on E. 55th St.
Return to the southeast corner of Broadway and 44th St.

17 Pokerino Palaces

In *The Town and the City* Kerouac uses the name of the Nickel-O Amusement Center to describe these predecessors of the modern pinball and video game parlors that are still found on Times Square. Of the Nickel-O he wrote: "there you have, at around four in the morning, the final scenes of disintegrative decay: old drunks, whores, queers, all kinds of characters, hoods, junkies, all the castoffs of bourgeois society milling in there, with nothing to do really but just stay there, sheltered from the darkness as it were." In the story Kerouac developed the idea that an atomic disease, virus X, was born in the Pokerino Palace which dissipated and destroyed all who entered. Eventually it would radiate and infect the entire world.
Walk through Times Square by heading north on Broadway and stop at the corner of 48th St.

18 Howard's Men's Clothing

In early 1949 Kerouac received an advance of $1000 from Harcourt Brace for *The Town and the City.* It was the first time he had received any gold for his writing. With the help of a friend, Tom Livornese, he went shopping for new clothes. They went to Howard's Men's Clothing Store at 1600 Broadway on the northeast corner of 48th St. and got a gray flannel suit, a burgundy sports jacket, shirts, and ties. The store is no longer in business, and gray flannel suits no longer the fashion for successful writers.
Walk one block north on Broadway and turn right one block east on 49th St. to the southeast corner of Seventh Ave.

19 Columbia Pictures

In 1944, after he left Columbia College, Kerouac took a series of odd jobs. He was hired as a script synopsizer for Columbia Pictures at 729 Seventh Ave. in a building that survives on the corner of W. 49th St. Kerouac would pick up a script here, read it, and condense it. (He mentions the job in *Vanity of Duluoz.*)
Go one block north on Seventh Ave. and stop between 50th St. and 51st St. On the east side of the street you'll see the old Taft Hotel building.

20   Taft Hotel

When William Burroughs first came to New York in 1939, he moved into the respectable Taft Hotel on Seventh Ave. at 50th St. Before long, the house detective caught him naked in bed with another man and he was kicked out. Later in a rooming house on Jane Street, Burroughs cut off his left little finger to prove his love for the same man. (He later wished he had it back.)

Taft Hotel.
Photo by Bill Morgan.

Walk one block west on 51st St. to Broadway and look at the Winter Garden Theater on the southeast corner.

21   Zanzibar

After Kerouac and his wife, Edie, returned from her family's home in Michigan in 1944, they resumed living near Columbia with Joan Adams, Allen Ginsberg, and the rest. Kerouac wrote some of the time and was taking too many drugs. He was working on a book called *The Sea Is My Brother* that was never to be published. In order to support them, Edie worked as cigarette girl at the Zanzibar Night Club at 1634 Broadway in the same building as the Winter Garden Theater, and at the 21 Club at 21 W. 52nd St. She fed Jack on steaks stolen from the kitchen. Edie didn't last long here and felt homesick for Michigan. (The Zanzibar is gone, but the 21 Club is still on the set.)
Walk north along Broadway for one block and turn left on W. 52nd St. Stop at the Virginia Theater at No. 245.

22   Guild Theater

In *Vanity of Duluoz* Kerouac went to see a play here with a football recruiter from Boston College. As a high school football star, Kerouac had been recruited by two major colleges, Columbia and Boston College. He was given a scholarship to Horace Mann, a prep school in the Bronx with close ties to Columbia. That didn't prevent Boston College from trying to get him to change his mind. According to Kerouac, Frances Fahcy, the coach of Boston College, met him at Times Square "and took me to William Saroyan's play *My Heart's in the Highlands,* and in the intermission when we went down to the toilet I'm sure I saw Rolfe Firney the Columbia man watching from behind the crowd of men." He felt that this was reported to Columbia's coach, Lou Little, and that it turned the coach against him. (The play ran in April of 1939 in the theater then called the Guild. Now it's called the Virginia.)

Guild Theater (now The Virginia).
Photo by Bill Morgan.

Return to Broadway, walk north for one block to the southeast corner of 53rd St. at No. 1678 Broadway.

23 Birdland

The great jazz genius Charlie "Bird" Parker was such a legend in his own lifetime that Birdland at 1678 Broadway was named for him. It opened in the basement in December of 1949. The owners were Morris and Irving Levy. In the early 1950s Kerouac visited and saw all the greats here, including George Shearing, Lee Konitz, and Lester Young. In *On the Road* Kerouac wrote about the night that he and Neal Cassady heard Shearing play. During the break Cassady pointed to the vacant seat on the stage and said, "God's empty chair." Shearing wrote the song "Lullaby of Birdland" inspired by this club. Such was the jazz from which sprang Kerouac's "spontaneous bop prosody." (The original Birdland closed in 1965.)

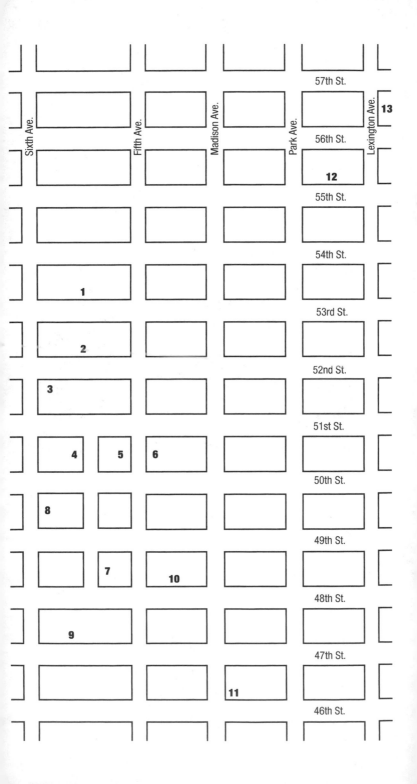

John Clellon Holmes "official" U.S Navy photograph, Samson, New York (Lake Geneva), August 1944.
©Allen Ginsberg Trust.

Rockefeller Center Midtown

Length of tour: 2-2 ½ hours
Subway: E or F to Fifth Avenue
Bus: M1, 2, 3, 4, 5, 27, 50 to Rockefeller Center
Begin this tour at the Museum of Modern Art on 53rd St. between Fifth and Sixth Ave.

1   Museum of Modern Art

Beginning in the 1960s, many of the Beats performed here in the continuing series of poetry readings hosted by Lita Hornick of the Kulchur Foundation. Of course, the Beats often came to see the exhibitions at MOMA. Poet Frank O'Hara worked his way up from gift shop clerk to curator. During his lunch breaks he wrote a se-

ries of poems that City Lights Books published in 1964 entitled
Lunch Poems.

Kerouac and Lucien Carr once visited MOMA to see the portraits by Modigliani, Carr's favorite modern painter. In May 1959
Kerouac and John Clellon Holmes saw a special screening here of
the film *Pull My Daisy.*

*From the Museum of Modern Art walk east on 53rd St. to the
corner of Fifth Ave., then south one block to 52nd St., turn
right onto 52nd St., and stop at No. 21.*

2   21 Club

The 21 Club at 21 W.
52nd St. opened in 1922
as a speakeasy. It became
synonymous with fash-
ionable high society dur-
ing the Prohibition and
Depression eras. Here in
1944, Edie Parker
Kerouac worked as a
cigarette girl while Ker-
ouac stayed home and
wrote (or goofed). If any
of the other Beats ever
entered these premises,
it wasn't reported by the
Club's star habitué,
Walter Winchell.

Continue west on 52nd   **21 Club.**
St. and stop anywhere   Photo by Bill Morgan.
before the next corner.

3   Three Deuces

It's hard to believe that this block of W. 52nd St. once housed dozens of the greatest jazz clubs in the city. Housed in old Victorian
brownstones, there were so many clubs that it was nicknamed
"Swing Street." During the 1930s and 1940s, the Onyx, the Famous
Door, Jimmy Ryan's, the Downbeat, Hickory House, and Kelly's
Stable were on this short block. Look at the signposts and you'll
see it has been renamed in honor of W.C. Handy, one father of the
blues. Kerouac's favorite club was the Three Deuces at 72 W. 52nd
St. Here he heard jazz greats Billie Holiday, Dizzy Gillespie,
Coleman Hawkins, Lester Young, Billy Eckstine, Charlie Parker,
saxophonist Ben Webster, and others not so great. On some nights

"Dizzy would take a bebop solo and Charlie would stand off and watch him. Then Charlie would take one and Dizzy would watch," according to Gilbert McKean.

Walk one block south on Sixth Ave. and turn left onto 51st St. On your right at the next small street you'll find No. 50, opening onto the side street of Rockefeller Plaza.

4 Rockefeller Center

In 1948-1949 Allen Ginsberg worked as copy boy for Associated Press Radio News Service, at 50 Rockefeller Center. (The Associated Press is still in the same building today.) Ginsberg's personal life was demanding full attention; at this point he was having visions of Blake in Harlem. He worked the midnight-to-8 a.m. shift. He was subletting his friend Russell Durgin's apartment at the time, and when Herbert Huncke stole some books, part of Ginsberg's wages went to compensate Durgin. Ten years later in the poem "My Sad Self" Ginsberg wrote "Sometimes when my eyes are red / I go up on top of the RCA Building / and gaze at my world, Manhattan . . . " (The RCA building is next to the Associated Press building and had an observation deck on the roof.)

Walk east on 51st St. to Fifth Ave. and look for 630 Fifth Ave. in the building on your left.

5 Passport Office

In *Desolation Angels* Kerouac wrote that Allen Ginsberg took him to the Passport Office here. Kerouac applied for a passport for his 1957 visit to Burroughs in Tangier. Outside they met Elise Cowen who was in love with Ginsberg and who would later commit suicide. Later that day near Union Square they ran into her again. If she was following him, Ginsberg didn't seem to notice.

Just across Fifth Ave. between 50th St. and 51st St. is Saint Patrick's Cathedral.

6 Saint Patrick's Cathedral

One of the places close to Kerouac's heart was Saint Patrick's Cathedral on Fifth Ave. at 49th St. Brought up a Catholic, he lovingly wrote of the beauty and mystery of the cathedral. In a letter to Cassady in 1951, Kerouac detailed one entire afternoon he spent here just "digging" the atmosphere and the people: "The church is the last sanctuary in this world. . . . Such lovely silence; such heights of mysterious upreaching darkness . . . " In *Visions of Cody* he wrote ". . . most striking of the windows and I didn't expect strikingness at this late hour — is at upper front left — a lonely icy congealed blue with streaks of hot pink . . . "

Saint Patrick's Cathedral.
Photo by Stacey Lewis.

Ginsberg stopped into Saint Patrick's on his way home from work in Rockefeller Center one morning and prayed for Neal Cassady. In "Howl" he wrote of those "who fell on their knees in hopeless cathedrals praying for each other's salvation and light and breasts, until the soul illuminated its hair for a second."
Return to the west side of Fifth Ave., head south to 49th St., and turn right. The building immediately to your left on the south side of 49th St. is No. 9 Rockefeller Center.

7   *Time Magazine*

Lawrence Ferlinghetti worked in the mail room of *Time Magazine* here at 9 Rockefeller Plaza in 1946. He had just gotten out of the Navy. After working here for eight months he quit and went to Columbia University for a Master's Degree on the G.I. bill, and eventually earned a *doctorate* from the Sorbonne in Paris. (He would later recall the minor havoc he and his co-workers wrought in the mailroom, forwarding editorial mail to random addresses; an early attempt at workplace subversion.) He later described the mail room crew as a "nose-picking gang of desperadoes." (*Time* editor Henry Grunwald mentions Ferlinghetti's passage through *Time* in his autobiography, *One Man's America.*)

Time and *Life* magazines were the source of much misinformation about the Beats in the 1950s. They repeatedly ran sensationalized stories about the degenerate lifestyles of the so-called "Beatniks," while ignoring the literary work of the writers. Kerouac, in particular, suffered from distorted reporting and the image that the popular media created of him as "Father of the Beats." (Grunwald saw things otherwise, and in his autobiography he defends *Time's* reporting on the Beats whom he says *Time* "took seriously." They may have taken them seriously, but Ginsberg's obituary in *Time's* April 1997 issue was condescending.
Walk west on 49th St. to the corner of Sixth Ave. and try to

stand back far enough from the northeast corner of the street to see the small building here.

8   Hurley's Saloon

Hurley's Saloon.
Photo by Bill Morgan.

In *Visions of Cody,* Kerouac wrote about following Lee Konitz, one of his favorite jazz musicians, after he came out of the bar (now called Hurley's Saloon) on the northeast corner of 49th and Sixth Avenue. "[The bar] is in a real old building that nobody ever notices because it forms the bebble at the hem of the shoe of the immense tall man which is the RCA Building — I noticed it only the other day while standing in front of Howard Johnson's eating a cone . . . New York is so immense that it would make no difference to anybody's ass if this building exists and is old."

After a stop for refreshments at Hurley's, stagger two blocks south on Sixth Ave. and turn left at the corner onto 47th St. Stop in the middle of the block at No. 41.

9   Gotham Book Mart

Founded by the erudite and astute Frances Steloff on January 1, 1920 at 128 W. 45th St., the Gotham Book Mart soon became a live center for the international avant-garde. It moved to 51 W. 47th St. in 1923, and in 1946 to its present address at 41 W. 47th St. (Its famous sign "Wise Men Fish Here," also moved, as did the wise

men.) Author Christopher Morley (who lived across the street at No. 46) and Mark Van Doren suggested the bookstore move to this small building owned by Columbia University to avoid landlord problems. In 1967, Andreas Brown became the principal owner.

Certainly the bookstore with the most prestigious literary reputation, Gotham carries an eclectic poetry stock with a special section by the Beats. There are also innumerable little

Gotham Book Mart.
Photo by Bill Morgan.

magazines and hard-to-find books by small presses. (They were also hard-to-find in the Gotham, due to its glorious disarray.) Upstairs there is a gallery for literary exhibitions and receptions, echoing with the loud and lusty voices of many literary generations.

The bookstore also hosted the James Joyce Society, with T.S. Eliot as the first member. Among the notables honored here at book parties have been Jean Cocteau, Anaïs Nin, Paul Goodman, Dylan Thomas, and William Carlos Williams. It could be said that one hasn't "arrived" until one has a book-signing at Gotham. Allen Ginsberg worked here for a few days. LeRoi Jones lasted slightly longer; this was his first job in New York City when he moved here from Newark in 1957. Numerous other authors have come and gone, some notable for their allergic reactions to clerical work. *Continue east on 47th St. to Fifth Ave., turn left one block to 48th St., and turn right. Stop at the large building called "Tower Forty-Nine."*

10　Sterling Lord

The office of literary agent Sterling Lord was at 15 E. 48th St. in 1957 when Jack Kerouac walked in. He was disgruntled with his own attempts to deal with publishers directly. Sterling Lord was just the man and he is still the agent for the Kerouac estate. (The building at this address has been torn down and replaced by the giant office tower, Tower Forty-Nine.)

Continue east to the corner of Madison Ave., turn south two blocks and stop at No. 383 at the corner of 46th and Madison.

11　Robert Giroux

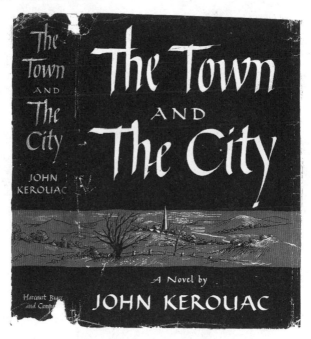

In 1949 Harcourt, Brace and Company published Kerouac's first book, *The Town and the City.* Kerouac's editor was Robert Giroux. Kerouac looked to Giroux as a literary mentor who could edit his books as Maxwell Perkins had edited Thomas Wolfe. Giroux did just that, up to a point. But after Giroux couldn't get Kerouac's second book published, the relationship lapsed. (One wonders, if Kerouac had lived, who would be his editor in today's corporate publishing jungle.)

Turn around and walk north on Madison Ave. to 55th St., turn right past Park Ave., and stop in front of what would have been No. 125 E. 55th St.

12   Carolyn Cassady

In the spring of 1943 Carolyn Robinson, later Carolyn Cassady, came to New York from Bennington College for one term. She was to work in New York at Dazian's Theatrical Fabric House. She studied draping at Traphagen School of Design, researched print

collections at the Metropolitan Museum of Art and the Museum of Modern Art, and attended performances of plays, opera, ballet. And she earned credit towards her degree in Stanislavsky drama. She lived here at 125 E. 55th St. and was a neighborhood air raid warden, as World War II raged. The building she lived in was replaced by the Phyllis and Lee Coffey Community House of Central Synagogue, now at 123 E. 55th St.

Carolyn Cassady, ca. 1943.
Courtesy of Carolyn Cassady.

Continue east on 55th St. to Lexington Ave. and turn left. Look for No. 681 on the east side of Lexington.

13   John Clellon Holmes

John Clellon Holmes, the author of the first Beat novel, *Go,* lived above the Dover Delicatessen at 681, apartment 4C on the fifth floor. This was when he first met Kerouac and Ginsberg. It is hard to picture this as a mainly residential neighborhood, but it once was. The building no longer stands; it's now an eyeglass store. In a 1948 letter Kerouac described Holmes' smoke-filled apartment as rugless with high ceilings. On one November evening in 1948 they began wondering how their generation would be remembered, if at all. They thought of the Lost Generation of the 1920s, and Kerouac said theirs was perhaps a "Beat Generation." In November 1952 Holmes used the term for the first time in print in the *New York Times Magazine.* He gave Kerouac credit for coining the name. As time went on, the original meaning of Beat as Kerouac saw it became perverted in terms like "beatnik." and Kerouac literally fled the scene.

Holmes threw many parties here, among them a very large one on April 20, 1949 when Kerouac's novel *The Town and the City* was sold to Harcourt Brace. In October of that year, Holmes gave a party for Ed White (a Denver friend of Neal Cassady) who was just home from Europe. Ginsberg and Kerouac began a giant collaborative poem to be spontaneously composed by everyone at the party, in the manner of the French Surrealists' "exquisite corpse." (Words on the wind, which later no one could remember.) Another frequent visitor those days was editor Jay Landesman, who published an early version of Ginsberg and Kerouac's *Pull My Daisy* in his *Neurotica* magazine in 1950. (Their neuroses were later also zanily displayed in Robert Frank's film version — much shown in the 1990s.)

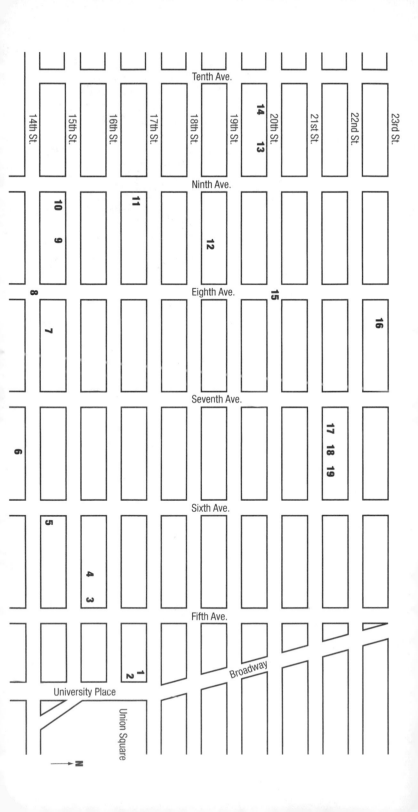

Hettie Jones.
Photo by Bela Ugrin. Courtesy of Hettie Jones.

Chelsea

Length of tour: 2 hours
Subway: 4, 5, 6, L, N, or R to Union Square
Bus: M1, 2, 3, 6, 7, or 18 to 14th St. or M14 to Union Square
Begin this tour on the northwest side of Union Square, near the corner of Broadway and E. 17th St.

1 *Partisan Review* / Allen Ginsberg

In 1958 Hettie Jones went to work as subscription manager for *Partisan Review* to support herself, LeRoi Jones, and their magazine, *Yugen.* By that time, *Partisan* had moved its offices to 41 Union Square West, and you'll see it just to the right of McDonald's near the corner of Broadway and E. 17th St. *Partisan Review,* a radical Leftist weekly, published writing by the leading thinkers of the day as well as poets T.S. Eliot, William Carlos Williams, and Robert Lowell. The magazine, begun in 1935 by the

John Reed Club, was taken over in 1937 by editors Philip Rahv and William Phillips and it rapidly became the most important journal of radical political analysis in the U.S., the equivalent of *Les Temps Modernes* in France. Hettie Jones tried to introduce writings by the Beats. *Partisan* did eventually publish Ginsberg, Frank O'Hara, John Ashbery, Kenneth Koch, and Lawrence Ferlinghetti, who made several appearances independently.

Allen Ginsberg had an office in this building throughout much of the 1990s. Under the direction of poet Bob Rosenthal, the office managed not only Ginsberg's day-to-day affairs of all kinds but also assisted many other poets and artists. Through Ginsberg's generosity, dozens of writers have received funds through his foundation. He was the poetic catalyst of his generation, and he charged the poetic consciousness of generations beyond his own, in many countries.

A few doors to the south of McDonald's is No. 33 Union Square.

2 Warhol's Factory

The Factory and *Partisan Review* offices.
Photo by Bill Morgan.

Andy Warhol's studio, The Factory, originally opened in 1963 at 231 E. 47th St., and then moved here to 33 Union Square West in February 1968. In 1974 Warhol moved to his last quarters at 860 Broadway, a block away to the north on the northeast corner of 17th St.

Several of Warhol's underground films were shot in this building, and here he created many of his most famous silkscreens. This was where underground film actress, Valerie Solanis, tried to kill Warhol on June 3, 1968. She was the sole member of SCUM [Society to Cut Up Men]. Although critically wounded, Warhol recovered but retained a tremendous fear of injuries and hospitals for the rest of his life. (He died of complications from a routine operation in a New York hospital in 1987.)

Walk south on Union Square West to the next corner and then one block west on 16th St. Turn left on Fifth Ave. and stop at No. 100.

3 National Opinion Research

Soon after graduating from Columbia University, Ginsberg began working in market research, public opinion surveys, and other short-term projects. In 1951, while at the National Opinion Research Corporation (affiliated with the University of Chicago) in this large office building at 100 Fifth Ave., he worked on an opinion survey about the Korean War. Several of his friends worked here during that period too: Carl Solomon and his wife, Olive, John Clellon Holmes, and Stanley Gould all coded questionnaires. In fact, Holmes was working here the day that Scribner's accepted his first novel, *Go*. He quit immediately.

Walk west on 15th St. to No. 27, about half a block towards Sixth Ave.

4 Thomas Wolfe

Wolfe was Kerouac's most important early literary influence. One of his reasons for coming to New York was because his literary hero had written *Look Homeward, Angel* here. Wolfe lived in this part of the city, wrote at various locations, and taught at New York University. In 1928 Wolfe moved into a room at the rear of the second floor in the brownstone at 27 W. 15th St. Here, surrounded by dirty clothes and dirty dishes, he finished writing *Look Homeward, Angel* on an ugly, heavy dining room table that he had

Thomas Wolfe's home, 1928.
Photo by Bill Morgan.

hauled into the apartment. (Years later, walking past, Kerouac still looked to Wolfe as his angel. Wolfe's *You Can't Go Home Again* also affected Kerouac. Sunk into alcoholism, and feeling he was losing his roots, he tried to return to live in his home town of Lowell, Mass. It was a sad return, proving the truth of Wolfe's title.)

Continue walking west on 15th St. and turn left onto Sixth Ave. Stop at the northeast corner of 14th St.

5   Living Theatre

Allen Ginsberg, Judith Malina, and Julian Beck at the opening of Allen's photography show, Holly Solomon Gallery, New York, 1984.
Photo by Ira Cohen. Courtesy of the Living Theatre.

After short stays at the Cherry Lane Theatre and uptown at 2641 Broadway, the Living Theatre settled into a home of its own. On October 19, 1958, it opened at 530 Sixth Ave. on the northeast corner of W.14th St., now the drab, yellow, four-story brick building on the corner. Formerly Hecht's Department Store, the old building took on a new radical life. The 162-seat theater was on the second floor, dressing rooms on the third. Founded on anarchist traditions by Julian Beck and Judith Malina, the Living Theatre was the most innovative and radical acting troupe in the city, a guerrilla theater that has lasted for decades. Here on January 13, 1959 they premiered William Carlos Williams' verse comedy, *Many Loves,* followed by Paul Goodman's *The Cave at Machpelah,* and Jack Gelber's *The Connection. The Connection* ran for over seven hundred performances in repertory. Although the critics panned the play, news spread by word of mouth that this was revolutionary theater. Later Kenneth H. Brown's *The Brig* enlarged the dissident repertory, followed by radical experimental plays by Jean Cocteau, Kenneth Koch, Michael McClure, Jackson MacLow, Frank O'Hara, and Philip Whalen. Many Beat poets read here to full houses. Kerouac gave a reading here in the spring of 1959. Kenneth Patchen and the Charles Mingus Jazz Workshop did an evening of poetry and jazz. Other poets included Ray Bremser, Edward Dahlberg, Lawrence Ferlinghetti, Allen Ginsberg, LeRoi Jones, Bob Kaufman, Frank O'Hara, and Peter Orlovsky. After presenting nine productions, the Living Theatre was padlocked by the IRS in October 1963 because of delinquent taxes. Beck and

Malina then took the whole company abroad, and it toured the Continent for years, with extended residences in Berlin, Paris, and Rome where they were much loved. (Not that they weren't often censored—they were busted in Avignon for obscenity in their production of *Paradise Now* and years later were thrown in jail in South America.) The Living Theatre's influence on European avant-garde theater was as great as its influence on modern American radical theater, if not greater, despite the McCarthyite repression of the IRS. Julian Beck died in 1985 but Judith Malina carries forward the great tradition.

Walk west on 14th St. to a building at No. 114, just on the other side of Sixth Ave.

6   Young Socialist League

The Young Socialist League offices were located in the five-story office building with the large glass windows at 114 W. 14th St. It hosted the first lecture ever given on Kerouac and his work. On April 6, 1958, Michael Harrington spoke on "The Kerouac Craze." He made a vigorous attack against Kerouac and the Beats, according to *Village Voice* reporter James Breslin. The musician-composer David Amram was there and defended Kerouac.

Continue walking along 14th St. for one and a half blocks until midway between Seventh Ave. and Eighth Ave. On the north side of the street is a small church.

7   Church of Our Lady of Guadalupe

Between Seventh and Eighth Avenues is the tiny Our Lady of Guadalupe, at 229 W. 14th St. When Kerouac was giving a series of poetry and jazz readings with poets Philip Lamantia and Howard Hart at the Circle in the Square they would come here daily for mass. All three had been raised as Roman Catholics.

Continue west to the corner of 14th St. and Eighth Ave.

Church of Our Lady of Guadalupe.
Photo by Bill Morgan.

8   Gregory Corso

In *Desolation Angels* Kerouac described a bar on the corner of
Eighth Ave. and 14th St. where Gregory Corso painted a mural.
The bar and mural are long gone, but the story remains that Corso
painted the mural with house paint for a few bucks. Kerouac describes the scene, "and the owners of the bar were big Italian
gangsters with gats. They stood around in loose-fitting suits as
Raphael [Corso] painted huge monks on the wall." According to
Kerouac, Corso spoiled the mural by slopping white paint all over
it, and Kerouac thought this proved Corso wasn't afraid of the
Mob. On the northeast corner at 80 Eighth Ave. is the tall office
building where New Directions Publishers offices are now located,
still the publisher of Dylan Thomas, Tennessee Williams, Ezra
Pound, William Carlos Williams, Corso, Robert Duncan, Denise
Levertov, Kenneth Patchen, Lawrence Ferlinghetti and many other
seminal writers.
Walk north one block; then turn left onto 15th St. and stop at
No. 322.

9   Paul Blackburn

In 1959 poet Paul Blackburn lived at 322 W. 15th St. in the four-
story brick building now housing El Cid Tapas Bar on the ground
floor. He described the scene in several of his poems, one of which
is entitled "Hot Afternoons Have Been in West 15th Street." Associated with the Black Mountain poets, Blackburn lived much of his
life in New York. Although he was one of the editors of the *Black*
Mountain Review, he never visited Black Mountain College. He
was the main organizer of poetry readings at East Village coffeehouses like Les Deux Megots and Le Metro Cafe in the 1960s, and
when the St. Mark's Poetry Project was founded, Blackburn helped
organize readings there until his death in 1971.
Continue walking west on 15th St. to No. 346.

10   Allen Ginsberg

In December 1951 Allen Ginsberg moved into several small furnished rooms at 346 West 15th St., where he stayed until October
1952. The rent was only $4.50 per week for the blue-painted attic
with dormer windows. Practically the whole block has undergone
restoration since the time Ginsberg lived here in what was then an
industrial part of town. The enormous Port Authority building
stands across the street.

     While living here, Ginsberg first met Gregory Corso at a bar in
the Village. Later, Kerouac was introduced to Corso in this apartment. Ginsberg wrote here and got into the nightlife around the

Village. At the San Remo bar, Ginsberg and Kerouac hung out with bohemians and what Kerouac called "subterraneans." Among Ginsberg's poems describing the apartment and neighborhood are "Marijuana Notation," "346 West 15th St.," and "A Ghost May Come." The following poem is from *Empty Mirror*.

Walking home at night,
reaching my own block
I saw the Port Authority
Building hovering over
the old ghetto side
of the street I tenement
in company with obscure
Bartlebys and Judes,
cadaverous men,
shrouded men, soft white
fleshed failures creeping
in and out of rooms like
myself. Remembering
my attic, I reached
my hands to my head and hissed,
"Oh, God how horrible!"

Walk to the corner of Ninth Ave. and turn right for two blocks. Stop in front of the large building with the porthole windows between 16th St. and 17th St.

11 National Maritime Union

The Union once occupied the end of the block between 346 W. 17th St. and 359 W. 16th St. where Covenant House now stands facing Ninth Ave. Lucien Carr, Henri Cru, Allen Ginsberg, Herbert Huncke, Jack Kerouac, and Carl Solomon were members of this union, and they came here to "ship-out" in the 1940s and 1950s. They spent a good deal of time hanging around the hall, waiting for ships going where they wanted to go. Although Kerouac shipped out more than once and Ginsberg made it to the Arctic Circle, they were essentially landlubbers out to earn some money and see the world, if not to get high on the high seas.

Coincidentally, Naomi Ginsberg, Allen's mother, worked here as a receptionist for Dr. Leon Luria, official doctor for the union. They had a short romantic relationship. When Ginsberg's brother Eugene was discharged from the service after World War II and enrolled in New York University's Law School, he now and then slept on the sofa in Dr. Luria's office. Down the street are the warehouses and docks from which seamen often shipped out. While Hettie Jones was working for *Partisan Review* she hired poet

Diane di Prima. When di Prima first found a copy of Ginsberg's "Howl" in the office, she took it down to the Hudson piers to read. *Go one block north on Ninth Ave. and turn right on W. 18th St. Stop at No. 319.*

12   Naomi Ginsberg

319 W. 18th St.
Photo by Bill Morgan.

In 1944 Naomi Ginsberg moved to the large, six-story brick building at 319 W. 18th St. She had a tortured history of mental illness. After her breakup with Louis Ginsberg she continued to be in and out of mental institutions. For a while she tried, unsuccessfully, to live with her sister. She moved to this apartment and found a job at the National Maritime Union around the corner. Allen Ginsberg, at the time a Columbia student, visited often and had his mail delivered here for a while. *Return to Ninth Ave. and turn right for two blocks. At 20th St. turn left and stop at No. 402.*

13   LeRoi and Hettie Jones

In the fall of 1958 LeRoi and Hettie Jones moved into this five-story building called the "Donac" at 402 W. 20th St. The once elegant, six-room parlor apartment faced the fenced courtyard of the Episcopal Seminary. Here they stayed until 1960. On any given night visitors might have included Kerouac, Ginsberg, Hubert Selby, Jr., Gregory Corso, Ray Bremser, John Wieners, Burroughs, Don Cherry, Ornette Coleman, Frank O'Hara, or Kenneth Koch. LeRoi Jones was writing *Cuba Libre* at the time. Through him the Beats

The "Donac."
Photo by Bill Morgan.

met many jazz and bebop legends. John Wieners, Max Finstein, and A.B. Spellman all stayed for extended periods as boarders.

Ginsberg introduced the Joneses to Ray Bremser's poetry and they had a big party for him at this apartment after he was released from prison. During the party, Kerouac and Larry Rivers took Bremser to Lucien Carr's apartment on Sheridan Square, and it was one of those Village nights that never seemed to end.

While living here the Joneses continued to edit *Yugen* magazine and Totem Press books. Diane di Prima's first book, *This Kind of Bird Flies Backward*, was published here in 1958 by Totem. At about the same time Totem teamed up with Ted Wilentz of the Eighth Street Bookshop and began publishing Totem/Corinth Books. Among others, they published Kerouac's *The Scripture of the Golden Eternity* and Philip Whalen's first full-length perspicacious rumination, *Like I Say*.

Continue west on 20th St. and near the end of the same block you'll find No. 454.

14   Jack Kerouac and Joan Haverty

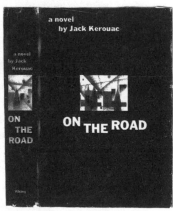

454 W. 20th St. House where Kerouac wrote *On The Road*.
Photo by Bill Morgan.

After living with Kerouac's mother for a few months, Joan Haverty, now the new Mrs. Kerouac, decided to move. She knew there was no way the marriage could last if they continued to live under the same roof with Jack's mother. In January 1951, Kerouac moved with her into this four-story, red brick rowhouse at 454 W. 20th St. Here, Kerouac stumbled upon the idea of typing on a long roll of teletype paper so that his thoughts could flow without stopping for paper changes. Between April 2 and April 22, 1951 he used teletype paper to write *On the Road*. Most of it was typed at this apartment, the rest at Lucien Carr's loft nearby.

A week after they moved in, Neal Cassady arrived in New York City. His departure for California shortly thereafter became the final scene in *On the Road*. Joan found a job working as a waitress at Stouffer's which gave Kerouac more time to write. Later he found a job working for Columbia Pictures as a script synopsizer. But before long the relationship between Jack and Joan deteriorated. In June when she told him she might be pregnant, he suggested she have an abortion. Joan chose to have the baby, and left the city to stay with her mother in Albany. Kerouac returned to his mother, now living in North Carolina.

Retrace your steps along 20th St. and continue east past Ninth Ave. to Eighth Ave. (Along the way you'll pass St. Peter's Episcopal Church, whose pastor was Clement Clarke Moore, the author of "A Visit from St. Nicholas," better known as "The Night Before Christmas.") When you reach the corner of Eighth Ave. and 20th St. stop and read about the next site.

15   Corner of Seventh Ave. and W. 20th St.

Look down 20th St. east towards Seventh Ave. That is the corner on which Dean Moriarity (Neal Cassady) and Sal Paradise (Kerouac) last see each other at the end of *On the Road*. Kerouac was on his way to a Duke Ellington concert in a Cadillac with Henri Cru, his school chum from Horace Mann. Cassady asked for a ride to Penn Station at 32nd St., but Cru said no. "So Dean couldn't ride uptown with us and the only thing I could do was sit in the back of the Cadillac and wave at him." (Later Cassady went on other roads with Ken Kesey and the Merry Pranksters in their bus with destination sign reading "Further.")

Turn north onto Eighth Ave., walk 3 blocks to 23rd St., and turn right. Stop at the Chelsea Hotel.

16   Chelsea Hotel

There are entire books written about the Chelsea and its counterculture inhabitants, here at 222 W. 23rd St. It was built in 1884 as one of New York's first co-op apartments and later became a hotel. The wrought iron balconies distinguish this building from all the others. Plaques near the front door honor former short- and long-term residents, among them Nelson Algren, Brendan Behan, Arthur B. Davies, James T. Farrell, Robert Flaherty, O. Henry, William Dean Howells, Julius Lester, Mary McCarthy, Edgar Lee Masters, Arthur Miller, Vladimir Nabokov, James Schuyler, John Sloan, Virgil Thomson, Mark Twain, Thomas Wolfe, and Yevgeny Yevtushenko. At the Chelsea Dylan Thomas fell into a coma after an evening of serious drinking at the White Horse Tavern. He did not go gently to his death in St. Vincent's Hospital.

More recently William Burroughs lived here, as did Gregory Corso, Herbert Huncke, Arthur Miller, Harry Smith, and the French poet Claude Pelieu. Lawrence Ferlinghetti passed through now and then. Andy Warhol made the place famous yet

William Burroughs, 1978.
Photo by Louis Cartwright.

again with his 1966 *Chelsea Girls,* filmed on location in these apartments. Bob Dylan wrote his "Sad-Eyed Lady of the Lowlands" while staying here. Other musicians have included Jimi Hendrix, Janis Joplin, Sid Vicious (who killed his girlfriend, Nancy Spungen, in a room here), The Grateful Dead, The Mamas and Papas, and The Jefferson Airplane. And there were artists like Willem de Kooning, Jackson Pollock, Larry Rivers, Alice Neal, and Mary Beach. Take time to read the memorials and look around the lobby at the art donated in lieu of tenant's rent, including some typical paintings of the New York School.

When you leave the Chelsea continue east on 23rd St. to Seventh Ave., and turn right. Head south for two blocks and turn left onto 21st St. Stop at No. 149.

17 Lucien Carr

In 1950-1951 Lucien Carr was living in a loft at 149 W. 21st St. It is the four-floor brownstone on the north side of the street that now has a café in the basement. Kerouac stayed here with Carr on several occasions and he wrote that he liked the "rolltop desk, bourbon, friends" at Carr's. Bill Cannastra lived in a loft a few doors down from Carr's and in the summer of 1950 they were continually visiting one another and giving a lot of parties. Cannastra's girlfriend at the time was Joan Haverty, who regarded him as something of a father figure. When Cannastra died in October 1950, Haverty moved into his vacant place. Only a few weeks after that Haverty and Kerouac were married and lived for a short while at the old Cannastra loft, then moved in with Kerouac's mother, and finally into a place of their own on W. 20th St. Later Jack left Haverty after she became pregnant with his daughter, Jan, and moved all his belongings here, where Allen Ginsberg and Liz Lehrman were also staying.

Continue east on 21st St. and stop a few doors away at No. 145.

18   Edwin Denby

Edwin Denby inhabited the fifth floor of this five-story brick warehouse building at 145 W. 21st St. from 1935 until his death in 1983. Well known as both a poet and a dance critic, his books include *Mediterranean Cities* and *Looking at the Dance.* In one of his

poems he wrote, "I myself like the climate of New York / I see it in the air up between the street / You use a worn-down cafeteria fork / But the climate you don't use stays fresh and neat." Among those who visited him here were W.H. Auden, Bertolt Brecht, Kurt Weill, Lotte Lenya, Rudy Burckhardt, Ginsberg, and Willem de Kooning.

Continue east on 21st St. to a parking lot, which was the location of No. 125.

Edwin Denby on his Chelsea rooftop, 1937.
Photo by Rudy Burckhardt.

19   William Cannastra

On the site of this lot at 125 W. 21st St. once stood a building where Bill Cannastra lived until the time of his death in October 1950. John Clellon Holmes describes the area in *Go.* "Agatson [Cannastra] lived in a drab district of warehouses, garment shops, and huge taxi-garages. His loft was at the top of an ugly brownstone, unoccupied but for a lampshade factory on the second floor. The halls smelled of burnt glue and bolts of cheap cloth, and the stairs above the factory floor were unlighted, narrow and treacherous with refuse. The loft itself was one of those floors-through with low windows, several grimy skylights that opened out on chimneys, and a sort of kitchen alcove at the back. It was always a fantastic litter of broken records, dusty bottles, mattresses, a slashed car seat, a few decrepit chairs from empty lots, and stray articles of ownerless clothing."

Cannastra's loft was infamous for the parties that often went on for several days. Cannastra was wild, to the point of madness—as a party trick he would eat glass. In *Go* Holmes remembers that "his dissipations, and the exploits accompanying them, were near-legendary." Many of the scenes were attended by Kerouac,

Ginsberg, Carr, Alan Ansen, and other subterraneans who hung out at the San Remo. After one of these parties, Cannastra challenged Kerouac to a naked race around the block in the rain. Cannastra stripped completely, but Kerouac followed with his shorts on. Another time while walking towards Sixth Ave., Cannastra began breaking off car radio antennas, and carrying them "forking out of his fingers like Jupiter's bolts of lightning." Ginsberg had Cannastra in mind when

William Cannastra (right).
©Allen Ginsberg Trust. Courtesy of Fahey/ Klein Gallery, Los Angeles.

he wrote in "Howl": "Who sang out of their windows in despair, fell out of the subway window ... cried all over the street, danced on broken wineglasses barefoot smashed phonograph records of nostalgic European 1930s German jazz finished the whiskey and threw up groaning into the bloody toilet, moans in their ears and the blast of colossal steamwhistles."

After Cannastra's horrible death in October 1950 on an IRT subway platform, his girlfriend, Joan Haverty, moved into his loft. Shortly thereafter Kerouac met her here, immediately fell in love with her and the very next day asked her to marry him. Haverty accepted after a few days and they were married on November 17, 1950 in Judge Vincent Lupiano's house in the Village. Kerouac had arranged a huge party of several hundred people at the loft on their wedding night, and it turned into a disaster as he passed out and had to be put to bed.

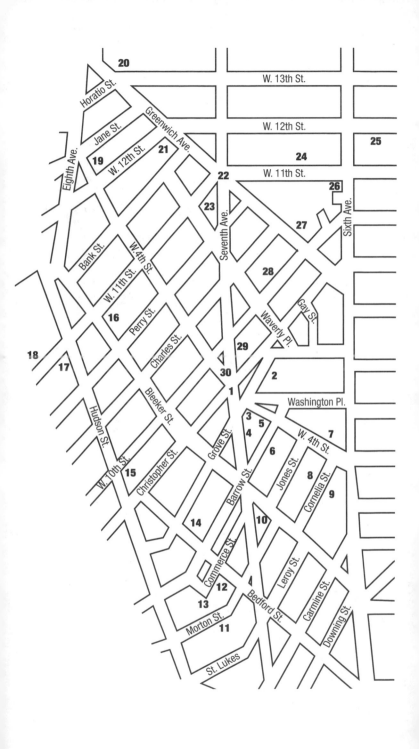

Allen Ginsberg, Lucien Carr, and William Burroughs on Sheridan Square, 1953.
©Allen Ginsberg Trust. Courtesy of Fahey/Klein Gallery, Los Angeles.

Greenwich Village
Tour 1

Length of tour: 2 ½-3 hours
Subway: No. 1 to Sheridan Square
Bus: M8, M10 to Sheridan Square
Begin this tour in Christopher Park near the subway stop at Seventh Ave., W. 4th St., and Christopher St. no earlier than noon, by which time the Village may have pulled itself together for the day.

1 Sheridan Square

Sheridan Square, which isn't a square, is the focal point of the West Village. (Other guide books will tell you that the park in which you see the statue of Civil War General Sheridan isn't technically Sheridan Square and that the little triangular shaped park further east on 4th St. is, but everyone considers this whole intersection to be Sheridan Square.)

Frank O'Hara wrote:
I was reflecting the other night meaning
I was being reflected upon that Sheridan Square
is remarkably beautiful, sitting in Jack
Delaney's looking out the big race-track window
on the wet
drinking a cognac while Edwin
read my new poem...

Jack Delaney's, which we'll visit in a few minutes, was on the corner of Grove and Seventh Ave. In Christopher Park, see George Segal's sculpture of two couples called "Gay Liberation." Gay and lesbian activists have often used this square as a rallying point, beginning with the Stonewall protests in June 1969. The Stonewall Bar is across the street from the park at 53 Christopher St., although in 1969 it was next door at No. 51.

Exit the tiny park onto Grove St. and stop at No. 92 near Waverly Place.

2   Lucien Carr

During the last half of the 1950s Lucien Carr lived in an apartment at 92 Grove St. It's a six-floor dark brick building with arches on the ground floor and tiny balconies that overlook the park. Kerouac stayed with Carr for weeks at a time. In 1955 he wrote to Ginsberg from here, "the windows wide open to the lyric of the Village trees rippling over girls with soft tits and boys with bicycles and junkies passing by and Stanley Gould going to the Riviera bar ... " In 1952 the park was a major drug dealing area in the Village.

In 1957 Kerouac wrote in *Desolation Angels* that Carr's "was the most beautiful apartment in Manhattan in its own Julien-like

92 Grove St.
Photo by Bill Morgan.

[Lucien-like] way, with a small balcony overlooking all the neons and trees and traffics of Sheridan Square, and a kitchen refrigerator full of ice cubes and Cokes to go with ye old Partners Choice Whiskey-boo." Once while Kerouac's girlfriend, Helen Weaver and Carr's wife, Cessa, talked in the apartment, the boys snuck down the fire escape to go to a bar. Kerouac fell and cut his head. "It's a ten-foot drop from that swinging fire escape to the sidewalk and as I fall I realize it but not soon enough, and turn over in my fall and fall right on my head."

On New Years Eve 1957, Carr had a quiet party here with Ginsberg, Peter Orlovsky, Elise Cowen, Joyce Glassman Johnson, and others. It was quite a contrast to the time Kerouac and Larry Rivers brought poet Ray Bremser here and made so much noise that the police came to break it up. Bremser was violating his parole by being in New York so he hid under the sofa until the police left.

Lucien Carr was working for United Press and lived here with his wife and two sons, Simon and Caleb. Simon is a painter and Caleb a writer whose recent book, *The Alienist,* made it to the bestseller lists in 1995. (If some Beats were alienated, their offspring often also were. Joyce Johnson's son, Daniel Pinchbeck, wrote about how they turned out in an issue of the *New York Times Magazine,* November 5,1995)

Walk back along the park on Grove to 4th St. and cross over to the tiny section of Grove St. behind the subway entrance. Here is the coffee shop that was once Jack Delaney's Steak House.

3   Jack Delaney's Steak House

Jack Delaney's Steak House at 72 Grove St. on Sheridan Square was an expensive restaurant visited by some of the Beat writers on special occasions. Kerouac and his father, Leo, went here to celebrate a Horace Mann football victory on Armistice Day 1939. It was the kind of place that both father and son could like. In *Vanity of Duluoz* Kerouac wrote, "So we go down to Jack Delaney's steak restaurant on Sheridan Square, myself little knowing how much time I was destined to spend around that square, in Greenwich Village, in darker years, but tenderer years, to come."

Directly ahead on Seventh Ave. and just around the corner to the left is the bar, The Garage, once called The Pad.

4   The Pad

The Pad, a new jazz club with a trendy name, featured Art Blakey and Charles Mingus in 1956. The bar at 99 Seventh Ave. South changed its name the following year to Lower Basin Street, with Dave Brubeck and George Shearing. Kerouac often spoke of how much he dug Shearing's music. Nowadays the club is called The Garage.

Retrace your steps to Sheridan Square, go around the corner of 4th St. to the east, and stop by the little triangular park in the center of 4th St. At the corner of Barrow and 4th St. is Sloan's supermarket which stands unknowingly on the site of the great Circle in the Square theater.

5 Circle in the Square/Louis' Tavern

The Circle in the Square theater was opened in 1951 at 5 Sheridan Square by Theodore Mann and José Quintero, staging plays such as Eugene O'Neill's *The Iceman Cometh,* Thornton Wilder's *Our Town,* and works by Tennessee Williams. Off-Broadway theater began here on the evening of April 24, 1952 when Geraldine Page opened in *Summer and Smoke.* It was the first theatrical success to originate anywhere but Broadway in over thirty years.

The theater also had a poetry series with a two-week gig of poetry and jazz by Kerouac, Philip Lamantia, and Howard Hart, accompanied by David Amram. Kerouac nervously read a selection of his own work and poems by Gregory Corso and Peter Orlovsky. At the break between sets the poets would go next door to Louis' Tavern, and often Amram had to begin the second set alone. To fill the time until they returned he began improvising and scatting. Sometimes the poets never did make it back for the second set, so the lighting man began playing and improvising with the lights, flashing them on and off, creating psychedelic effects like the light shows to come ten years later. Over the years Amram has continued to improvise words to music. (In 1972 the building was torn down to make way for the giant apartment building now on the site, and the theater moved uptown.)

At the corner of Barrow to the left of the Circle in the Square was Louis' Tavern.

In the late 1950s Louis' Tavern, at 196 W. 4th St., was located below street level and had a house special of spaghetti and meatballs with tomato and lettuce salad for 65 cents. It replaced the San Remo as the local hangout for many of the Beats. Other regulars were artists or actors from the Circle in the Square next door. James Dean, Steve McQueen, Jason Robards, and William Styron were among the irregular regulars.

Go down Barrow towards Seventh Ave. to No. 15.

6 Ted Joans/Café Bohemia

In the early 1950s, poet Ted Joans lived in a tiny room at 4 Barrow St. His room had space for one single bed and not much more. When his neighbor, Ahmed Basheer, lost his place, he moved in with Joans. Since Basheer was putting up Charlie Parker at the time, Parker also moved in. In an interview Joans said, "We used to even take turns. Bird said, 'I don't come in till 3 or 4 in the morning — you cats should get up and let me sleep'." (They did, he did.)

Progressive jazz animated the Café Bohemia at 15 Barrow St. The Bohemia showcased Cannonball Adderley, Miles Davis, Charles Mingus, and Randy Weston. Although it was a little expensive, Kerouac loved going to the Bohemia. He went to hear Wig Walters, and wrote Burroughs about him: "He is however a serious jazz artist and was wailin on bass with a gang of new musicians who are the wave of the future."

LeRoi Jones dropped by here to listen to John Coltrane and Miles Davis. Diane di Prima described seeing Miles at the Café Bohemia, "slick and smart as they come, exchanging sets with Charlie Mingus, cool then and cool now." The Café Bohemia is now the Barrow St. Ale House, still in the same converted 19th-century stable.

Return to 4th St., turn right, and walk two short blocks to the east. As you pass Jones St. on the right, look up the street. This is where the photo for Dylan's album The Freewheelin' Bob Dylan *was taken. Stop at No. 161 almost at the corner of Sixth Ave.*

7 Bob Dylan

Bob Dylan's apartment.
Photo by Bill Morgan.
Bob Dylan and Suze Rotolo on W. 4th St.
Courtesy of Columbia Records.

After moving out of the Hotel Earle in 1961, Bob Dylan stayed in the four-story brick building at 161 W. 4th St. near Sixth Ave. He found a two-room apartment here and stayed through 1962 while performing at Gerde's Folk City on the other side of Washington Square Park. While living here, he recorded songs like "Positively 4th St."

Continue east on 4th St. to the next street on the right, Cornelia St. Turn right to No. 7.

8   W.H. Auden

The British poet W.H. Auden (whose face was once described as a wedding cake left out in the rain and run over) lived in the rather modernized-looking building at 7 Cornelia St. from 1945 until 1953, when he moved to St. Mark's Place. Auden was at the top of his fame during those years, lecturing and reading around the world. Here he wrote *The Age of Anxiety* and *Nones*. Auden's secretary during part of this period was Alan Ansen, who became a friend of Bill Cannastra and through him met Allen Ginsberg, Gregory Corso, Kerouac, and William Burroughs. Although cordial to the Beats, Auden never seemed to really appreciate their work. It was as if his eyes and ears also had the Oxbridge accent.

Auden and his longtime companion, Chester Kallman, composed the libretto for Igor Stravinsky's *The Rake's Progress* here. Stravinsky frequently came to dinner at Auden's during the work on the opera. Auden told him a long story about keeping track of a mouse that had been eating off his dirty dishes. Stravinsky wondered if the plates he was eating from had been adequately washed before their dinner. (Nevertheless, the *Rake* progressed.) *Walk a few steps south to No. 18 on the other side of the street.*

9   Phoenix Bookshop

The Phoenix Bookshop was founded in the 1950s at 18 Cornelia St. On March 23, 1962 the fourth owner, Larry Wallrich, sold the works to Bob Wilson. Much later, in 1973, Wilson moved the store around the corner to 22 Jones St. In 1963, Ed Sanders' *Fuck You* magazine and Ted Berrigan's *C* were produced here on a mimeo machine. Diane di Prima printed the first issues of *The Floating Bear* on the Phoenix mimeo. The Phoenix, one of the very best bookstores in the city for modern poetry, also published a beautiful series of chapbooks by W.H. Auden, Amiri Baraka, Diane di Prima, Gary Snyder, Allen Ginsberg, Gregory Corso, Michael McClure, Marianne Moore, and others. (Unfortunately, the Phoenix is no longer rising, having closed after 40 years.)
Continue to Cornelia St. and Bleecker St., turn right (west) on Bleecker one short block, and left on Morton St. Stop at No. 7.

10   LeRoi Jones and Hettie Jones

LeRoi Jones and Hettie Cohen Jones first lived together in a one-and-a-half-room apartment on the top floor of 7 Morton St. in the old Italian neighborhood near Bleecker. Hettie Cohen found Apt. 20 listed in the *Village Voice* as "semiprofessional and semifurnished." It was up five flights of stairs, with white brick walls and Manhattan's smallest bathtub. She met LeRoi when she

interviewed him for a job at
Record Changer magazine in a
storefront at 171 Sullivan St. (He
was hired!) In the Morton Street
apartment in 1958 they first
published *Yugen*, one of the
seminal little magazines of the
period. To celebrate the first issue, they had a giant party with
a keg of beer from the nearby
A&M Beer Distributors. They
were married on October 13,
1958, and later that year moved
uptown to W. 20th St. The building hasn't changed much since
they breathed here. The old

7 Morton St.
Photo by Bill Morgan.

front door (through which passed many a poet to oblivion or
fame) is the same.
Continue west on Morton St. across Seventh Ave. to No. 48.

11   David Kammerer

In 1943 David Kammerer lived in the restored brick townhouse at
48 Morton St. Around Christmas-time 1943, Lucien Carr brought
Ginsberg here to meet Kammerer, and that evening Ginsberg first
met Burroughs. Kammerer lived here until August 1944, when he
was murdered by Lucien Carr. *New York* magazine later called the
incident "The Columbia Murder That Gave Birth to the Beats."
(For more details see Columbia University tour, site 4)

   Chandler Brossard lived in the building and knew Kammerer
and Burroughs (who lived around the corner on Bedford St).
Brossard once took them out to dinner at a French restaurant, Au
Bon Pinard. Brossard was writing for the *New Yorker*'s "Talk of the
Town" column. His first novel, *Who Walk In Darkness*, plumbed
the depths of the subterranean culture of 1940s Greenwich Village. Brossard is sometimes mentioned as one of the first Beat
novelists, but he objected to such characterization. Their talk
never showed up in his column. They were not the *New Yorker*'s
type of New Yorker.
Retrace your wavering steps back to Bedford St. and turn left.
Just around the corner stop at No. 69.

12   William Burroughs

William Burroughs lived in the front second-floor apartment at
69 Bedford in 1943 and 1944. Burroughs arrived from Chicago

with his friend, David Kammerer, who was following Lucien Carr. Burroughs, Carr, and Kammerer made a hell-raising trio. Once Carr broke off a piece of his beer glass with his teeth. Kammerer followed suit and this prompted Burroughs, always the good host, to bring them a tray of razor blades and lightbulbs from the kitchen. Kerouac said that this was his "first glimpse of the Real Devil (the three of em together)." When Carr came here the morning after Kammerer's murder and offered Burroughs a cigarette from the dead man's bloody pack, Burroughs advised him to get a good lawyer.

Ginsberg and Kerouac came here often. On Kerouac's first visit, Burroughs gave him a copy of Spengler's *Decline of the West* along with the advice, "Edify your mind, my boy, with the actuality of fact." In Burroughs' day guests would have entered the building down a flight of steps similar to those on the buildings to the immediate left.

Continue along Bedford to the next corner and turn left onto Commerce St. Stop at the theater at No. 38, just before the bend in the street.

13   Cherry Lane Theatre

The Cherry Lane Theatre at 38-42 Commerce St. was founded in 1924. In December 1951 the Living Theatre first produced Gertrude Stein's *Doctor Faustus Lights the Lights* here. William Carlos Williams was in the audience and wrote to the founders, Julian Beck and Judith Malina, that the play was "so far above the level of commercial theatre that I tremble that it might fade and disappear."

The Living Theatre also staged here Kenneth Rexroth's *Beyond the Mountains,* Gertrude Stein's *Ladies Voices,* T.S. Eliot's *Sweeney Agonistes,* Pablo Picasso's *Desire Trapped by the Tail,* Paul Goodman's *Faustina,* Alfred Jarry's *Ubu the King,* and John Ashbery's *The Heroes.* The poets Frank O'Hara and John Ashbery doubled as actors. On February 24, 1952, Dylan Thomas read his poetry here and went to the White Horse Tavern afterward with Malina, Beck, and most of the cast of the Living Theatre.

LeRoi Jones' savage incisive one-act play *Dutchman* opened here on January 12, 1964, and won an Obie for best play of the 1963-1964 season. Jennifer West played the white woman who acted out her eroticism on the subway, and Robert Hooks played a black man stabbed and thrown from the train.

Walk around Commerce St. to your right, go right again on Barrow, and then left on Bedford. Stop at No. 86.

14 Chumley's

After the White Horse Tavern, the oldest literary watering hole in the Village is certainly Chumley's, at 86 Bedford St. It has always attracted a bohemian crowd to its small, cozy rooms even though there is no sign outside. No one would suspect that behind the rather formidable door with the metal grate is a warm, friendly tavern. Opening in 1928, Chumley's began as a speakeasy during Prohibition, and forever after felt the need not to advertise itself. There is another exit out the back way, used for quick escapes during Prohibition days. (Later, the patrons used it for other escapades.) Over the years it was frequented by writers like Theodore Dreiser, Edna Ferber, F. Scott Fitzgerald, Mary McCarthy, Edna St. Vincent Millay, Anaïs Nin, Eugene O'Neill, J.D. Salinger, Upton Sinclair, and Orson Welles. William Burroughs and David Kammerer liked to start an evening here with dinner during the early 1940s. Unbeknownst to them, a straight Lawrence Ferlinghetti might have been seen drinking wine in a corner. Chumley's was his favorite place in the Village in those days, as was Marie's Crisis, off Sheridan Square. On the walls you'll find book covers by various Beat writers who hung out there now and then.

Follow Bedford St. to Christopher St., turn left and walk west on Christopher St. to Hudson St. Turn right on Hudson one block to 10th St. and turn right again. Stop at No. 240.

15 Howard Hart

During the late 1950s Kerouac stayed often with Howard Hart, a poet and jazz drummer, who had done the first poetry and jazz reading in New York with Dave Amram at the Brata Gallery on E. 10th St. Hart lived in the six-story red brick apartment house at 240 W. 10th across from the police station.

On one occasion, a drunken Kerouac was beaten up near the San Remo by an ex-marine boxer, who cut his face with a silver ring and broke his nose and arm. Kerouac staggered to Hart's apartment. Hart, Leroy MacLucas, and Philip Lamantia took him to the emergency room of St. Vincent's Hospital. Another time Joyce Glassman Johnson had to take Kerouac to the emergency room after a fight outside the same bar.

Jack Micheline also lived in this building in 1957 and ran into Kerouac many times at Hart's apartment. Micheline was a thirsty proletarian poet, who had just won the "Revolt in Literature Award" at the Half Note Jazz Club for poems that would appear in his book *River of Red Wine*. Micheline continued to drink from that river but moved west and took up permanent residence in San Francisco.

Continue in the same direction on 10th St. to Bleecker St. Turn left and stop at No. 393.

16   Mark Van Doren

Mark Van Doren, a profound critic and brilliant professor at Columbia for 40 years, won the
Pulitzer Prize for Poetry in 1940
for his *Collected Poems*. In the
1940s he lived in the dark gray,
four-story brick townhouse at
393 Bleecker. He had been enthusiastic about Kerouac's *The
Town and the City*, for which he
wrote a blurb calling Kerouac
"wiser than Thomas Wolfe." As
for *Doctor Sax,* Van Doren
judged the book "monotonous
and probably without meaning
in the end." Kerouac came here
to pick up the condemned
manuscript.

Mark Van Doren's house.
Photo by Bill Morgan.

*Continue along Bleecker to W.
11th St. and turn left. On the
next corner across Hudson St.
is the White Horse Tavern.*

17   White Horse Tavern

The most famous literary bar in the Village is the White Horse
Tavern at 567 Hudson. Built in 1880, it's one of the few wood-
framed buildings remaining in this district. The great Welsh poet
Dylan Thomas drank oceans of ale here in the 1950s, as well as on
the night he died of it. He made the White Horse famous, but
many other great writers drank here, including Norman Mailer,
William Styron, Vance Bourjaily, Frederic Morton as well as
Lawrence Ferlinghetti and other New Directions authors. (The
publisher of New Directions, James Laughlin, had an elegant little
apartment at 9 Bank St. in the West Village, not too far from the
White Horse, and his favorite authors often stayed there.)

Kerouac hung around the White Horse, too. He was living with
Helen Weaver across the street. He drank heavily and was eighty-
sixed from the White Horse several times. Once he found "Kerouac
go home!" scrawled on the men's room wall. (He didn't go.) In *Desolation Angels* he described this scene: He was visiting his ex-girl-
friend, Helen Weaver, when his new girlfriend, Joyce Glassman, de-

manded he meet her at the White Horse. Joyce "drags me out forc-
ibly as if by the hair, to a cab to her home, from which I learn: Alyce
Newman [Glassman] is not going to let anybody steal her man from
her, no matter who he will be. And I was proud."

The old wooden barroom has barely changed since Kerouac's
day; a few extra side rooms have been added and in the summer
they have outdoor seating for those who can't stand up any longer.

White Horse Tavern.
Photo by Bill Morgan.

*Turn left as you stagger from the White Horse and stop just
around the corner on 11th St. in front of No. 307. (It's inside
the little courtyard just across 11th St. from the White Horse.)*

18   Helen Weaver

Kerouac's girlfriend in 1956 and 1957, Helen Weaver, lived on the
third floor of 307 W. 11th St. with Helen Elliott, a former girlfriend
of Lucien Carr's. They called them the "Two Helens." Helen Elliott
had a large dog named Treff. Once Kerouac and Carr took the dog
to the bar and sent Helen a note, "Help, I'm trapped with Treff in
the White Horse—come rescue."

In *Desolation Angels* Kerouac says this apartment was his first
stop when he returned from Mexico with Ginsberg, Peter
Orlovsky, and Orlovsky's brother, Lafcadio. Arriving just after a
snowfall, they called up to the window of the Two Helens (named
"the two Ruths" in the book): "But when we stand there and yell
up at cute Chelsea District Dickensian windows (our mouths
blowing fog in the icy sun) they stick their two pretty brunette
heads out and see the four bums below surrounded by the havoc
of their inescapable sweatsmelling baggage." The Two Helens let
the tired travelers stay with them. Ginsberg and the Orlovskys

eventually found places of their own, and Kerouac stayed on in Helen Weaver's room.

Return to Hudson and walk north. Bear right onto Eighth Ave. just past the playground on the right side of the street and turn right one block later onto W. 12th St. At the next corner, turn left on W. 4th St. and stop at No. 323.

19   Lucien Carr

Lucien Carr lived in an apartment at 323 W. 4th St. In March 1953 Ginsberg stayed there while Carr was in Mexico. (Look at the street signs on the corner and you'll see why Greenwich Village is an easy place to get lost in: You're standing at the corner of W. 12th and W. 4th Streets.)

Continue to the next corner on W. 4th St. and turn right at the Corner Bistro onto Jane St. At the next corner make a left turn to Greenwich Ave., then a quick turn right to W. 13th St. Stop at No. 235.

20   Lawrence Ferlinghetti

Although a San Franciscan for over forty years now, Lawrence Ferlinghetti was born in South Yonkers and lived in the New York area and Westchester for many years. After World War II, as a graduate student at Columbia University on the G.I. Bill, he lived in the Village at 235 W. 13th St. with Ivan R. Cousins, Jr. The red brick building is still here. Later in the summer of 1946 they moved to E. 26th St. near Bellevue Hospital, while Ferlinghetti worked in the mailroom of *Time* magazine. It was a coldwater flat at basement level, and they called it "Burglarstop." They painted the walls bright yellow with Kemtone paint, ate a lot of canned spaghetti, drank much red wine, and usually ended up weekend evenings at Marie's Crisis or Chumley's.

Retrace your steps to Greenwich Ave. and stop near the movie theater on the corner of W. 12th St.

21   Greenwich Theater

Leo Percepied and Mardou Fox [Jack Kerouac and Alene Lee] in *The Subterraneans* broke up for good after seeing a movie at the Greenwich Theater at 97 Greenwich Ave. In September 1953, Kerouac and Lee walked over from Avenue A to see *The Brave Bulls* starring Mel Ferrer. Kerouac wrote on the next-to-last page of *The Subterraneans*, "I cried to see the grief in the matador when he heard his best friend and girl had gone off the mountain in his own car, I cried to see even the bull that I knew would die and I knew the big deaths bulls do die in their trap called bullring." The

book ends with this: "In
the movie I hold her hand,
after a fifteen-minute wait,
not thinking to at all not
because I was mad but I
felt she would feel it was
too subservient at this
time to take her hand in
the movieshow, like lovers."
But their relationship was
over and Kerouac went
home to his mother's place
in Queens and wrote *The
Subterraneans.*
***Continue on Greenwich
Ave. to the corner of
Seventh Ave.***

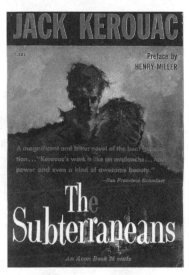

22 Loew's Sheridan Theatre/Esoteric Records/ St. Vincent's Hospital

One block north at 12th St. stood Loew's Sheridan Theatre until
the new addition to the hospital was built. In 1958 a historic concert took place here, with Billie Holiday and the Modern Jazz
Quartet. Holiday's cabaret license had been revoked in 1949 due to
her heroin use, and the only time she performed after that was at
this concert and a few others at Carnegie Hall. Ginsberg, Kerouac,
Neal Cassady, John Clellon Holmes, and other Beats had heard
Billie Holiday perform in the 1940s in Harlem and on 52nd St.,
and most of them came to hear her here at the Sheridan.

St. Vincent's Hospital occupies several buildings around this corner. Kerouac was brought here after a boxer beat him up. The doctors patched him up and gave him medication to help him stop
drinking. This is the same hospital where Dylan Thomas died in an
alcoholic coma in 1953, and where poet James Schuyler died in
1990. It is also where Gregory Corso first appeared in the world on
March 26, 1930, much to everyone's delight and astonishment.

Jerry Newman, who owned Esoteric Records at 75 Greenwich Ave.
near this corner, employed writer Seymour Krim as a clerk. He had
been a classmate of Kerouac's at Horace Mann. The large brick building that housed Esoteric Records still stands near the corner of
Greenwich and Seventh Ave.; the shop was where the newsstand and
Greenwich Flower Shop are now. In 1951 Kerouac wrote Cassady, and
described a party in the back room of the Esoteric Record Shop with
Milton 'Mezz' Mezzrow, jazz clarinetist. In 1955 Kerouac hoped to

make a recording of *On the Road* at Jerry Newman's studio here, with Allen Eager on tenor, but it was never done.
Walk a block south on Seventh Ave. and stop by the Village Vanguard at No. 178.

23   Village Vanguard

Jack Kerouac at the Village Vanguard, 1957.
Courtesy of Edie Kerouac Parker Estate.

The Village Vanguard, in the basement of 178 Seventh Ave. South, is still *the* place for Jazz in the Village. Opened in 1934 and relocated here in 1935 by Max Gordon, this nightclub's roster reads like the Entertainment Hall of Fame; it would probably be easier to list the musicians who didn't play here. Among those who did were John Coltrane, Miles Davis, Dizzy Gillespie, Woody Guthrie, Coleman Hawkins, Leadbelly, Charles Mingus, Thelonious Monk, Charlie Parker, Art Tatum, and Sarah Vaughan.

The Beat writers would have come here much more often had it not been so expensive. Kerouac said, "you've got to have mucho money" to visit the Vanguard. Kerouac did a series of readings here on seven consecutive nights in December of 1957 with the J.J. Johnson Quartet as the warm-up act. Kerouac was smoking and drinking a lot to ease his nerves. *Tonight Show* host, Steve Allen, came more than once, and he and Kerouac made a beautiful poetry and jazz record together. But other critics weren't so enthralled. They anathematized his lifestyle, put down his writing, and scoffed at his performance style. Kerouac's need to drink to overcome his acute shyness didn't help him onstage, and the readings were a critical flop. (Now the recordings of it are much prized.)

Return to the corner of Greenwich Ave. and cross over to W. 11th St. Go east towards Sixth Ave. and stop at No. 123 W. 11th St.

24 The Fifties

Robert Bly eclectically edited his literary magazine, *The Fifties*, in his apartment at 123 W. 11th St. At decade's change, the magazine became *The Sixties*. The magazine published much poetry in translation and works by the "deep image" poets, among others. In the 1950s work by Gary Snyder, Robert Creeley, Denise Levertov, and Charles Olson appeared regularly. The editorial sentiments of the magazine were strictly against the Beats however. An ad for the magazine stated that the reader would never find anything that sounded like it was written by William Burroughs or LeRoi Jones, and Allen Ginsberg was placed in the "Wax Museum" for his lack of poetic images. At one time they rated Charles Olson's *Maximus Poems* as "the worst of the year." Bly saw Denise Levertov often while he was living here. W.S. Merwin, Galway Kinnell, and James Dickey also often visited Bly who much later was to become the super-popular guru of a men's movement. (His book *Iron John* became a national bestseller in 1990-1991.)
Continue on W. 11th St. to Sixth Ave., turn left for one block, then turn right on W. 12th St., and stop at No. 66.

25 The New School

The New School for Social Research in this Bauhaus-inspired building at 66 W. 12th St. was founded in 1919 as a highly alternative means of higher education. It was a refuge for European intellectuals fleeing the Second World War, and many great scholars taught here. The G.I. Bill enabled several Beat writers to attend classes here after the war. In 1949, Kerouac and John Clellon Holmes took a course from Meyer Schapiro on the Impressionists, a course from Alfred Kazin on *Moby Dick*, and several courses in literature taught by Elbert Lenrow. Anatole Broyard also attended under the G.I. Bill. Bob Kaufman was an erratic student here in the 1940s and met Ginsberg and Burroughs. Judith Malina took a dramatic workshop from the great German director Erwin Piscator. Tuli Kupferberg did graduate work, and Lenore Kandel, author of *The Love Book*, went to the New School before going west in the late 1950s. Others in the avant-garde taught here as well: John Cage, Alan Watts, Hettie Jones, LeRoi Jones, Frank O'Hara, and W.H. Auden.
Return to Sixth Ave. and turn left. Walk a block south and stop at No. 461 Sixth Ave.

26 David Amram

For thirty-seven years, jazz musician David Amram lived in an apartment above the Chinese restaurant at 461 Sixth Ave. From 1959 until early 1996, many jazz greats spent quality time here. Amram, who had done some early performances with Kerouac, Philip Lamantia, and Howard Hart at the Circle in the Square, worked on the score for the Robert Frank and Alfred Leslie film, *Pull My Daisy*, when he was living in this building. Amram's auto-biography, *Vibrations*, was also set in motion here.

Continue south on Sixth Ave. to 10th St. and turn right. Stay on the right side of 10th and midway on the block between Sixth Ave. and Greenwich Ave. you'll see a little alleyway with a gate called Patchen Place. It's easy to miss. Here at one time lived major poet e.e. cummings, radical journalist John Reed ("Ten Days That Shook the World"), and Djuna Barnes (one of the finest prose writers of the century). Her novel "Nightwood"is a great expatriate text. While still a student, Lawrence Ferlinghetti tried to meet e.e. cummings here but couldn't get past his wife, Marion. He did meet Djuna Barnes through their publisher New Directions, and had coffee with her at the Rienzi on MacDougal. There was a heavy rain that day, and Ferlinghetti escorted her home under her umbrella, but wasn't allowed in. Young, heterosexual poets weren't her specialty. Continue on 10th St. to Greenwich Ave. and at the corner turn right to the second building on the north side of the street, No. 22.

27 *Village Voice*

The *Village Voice* was first issued on October 26, 1955, and edited in rooms above Sutter's Bakery at 22 Greenwich Ave. That's the tiny, three-story building with large picture windows. Edwin Fancher was the publisher, Daniel Wolf the editor, and Norman Mailer a co-owner in the early days. The newspaper soon became a liberal voice for the entire city, not just the Village. Its impressive staff included Jonas Mekas as film critic, Berenice Abbott and Fred McDarrah as photographers, Frank O'Hara as art critic, and Norman Mailer, Nat Hentoff, and Don McNeill as columnists.

The *Village Voice* ran this ad on December 2, 1959: "Add Zest To Your Tuxedo Park Party ... Rent a Beatnik! Completely equipped: Beard, eye shades, old Army jacket, Levis, frayed shirt, sneakers or sandals (optional). Deductions allowed for no beard, baths, shoes or haircuts. Lady Beatniks also available, usual garb: all black (Chaperone required)." The rental service was the brainstorm of someone on the *Voice* staff, and for a while poet Ted Joans rented himself out, eventually earning enough to book passage on a ship to France from where he didn't return for decades. Ted Joans now carries on his "Teducation" in Seattle, much to the poetic enlightenment of that hinterland.

Go back to 10th St. and walk west on 10th to No. 139.

28   Ninth Circle Bar

In 1960 William Smith was the self-proclaimed "Beatnik Candidate for President" and often hung-out at the Ninth Circle Bar at 139 W. 10th St. (John F. Kennedy edged him out.) This is also the bar where Edward Albee saw the words "Who's afraid of Virginia Woolf?" written in soap on the restroom mirror. The bar is now called Caffé Torino. (Enter the restroom and write your own answer to the original question in soap.)

Continue west along 10th St. to Seventh Ave. Stop near the building on the southeast corner, at present known as the Night Gallery café.

29   Nick's Jazz Club

In 1940, student Kerouac came to Nick's Jazz Club at 170 W. 10th St. and Seventh Ave. South to interview George Avakian for the Horace Mann school newspaper. Avakian was a music critic and a jazz authority and gave Kerouac his first in-depth lesson on the history of the music.

Stop directly across Seventh Ave. at the Café Riviera.

30   Café Riviera

The Café Riviera at 225 W. 4th St. on the corner of Seventh Ave. South was one of the new bars Kerouac liked to go to in 1955. Kerouac met some of his subterranean friends here, but by the late 1950s they were becoming too critical of him. His old Horace Mann pal, Henri Cru, was the bouncer here. Kerouac said "Henri is a wonderfully interesting raconteur and bon vivant and regular good man who however thinks that he must take possession of me, soul, body, heart, all of it, or none at all." The café was a magnet for bohemians and others who had nothing to do but become great artists and writers.

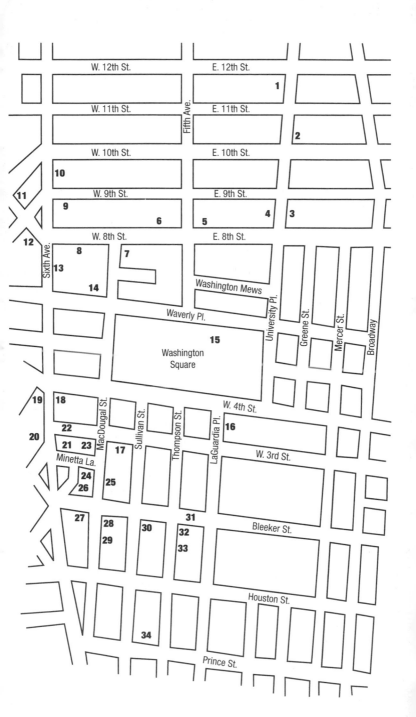

William Burroughs and Alan Ansen at the San Remo.
©Allen Ginsberg Trust. Courtesy of Fahey/Klein Gallery, Los Angeles.

Greenwich Village
Tour 2

Length of tour: 3 ½-4 hours
Subway: 4, 5, 6, L, N, or R to Union Square
Bus: M2, 3, 5, or 18 to 14th St. or M14 to University Place
Begin this tour on the west side of University Place between E. 11th and E. 12th St. (You might want to break the tour into two sections and end the first part at Washington Square.)

1 Frank O'Hara/Cedar Tavern

In 1957 the poet and art curator Frank O'Hara moved to 90 University Place, an old, three-story red brick building. Here he stayed until 1959, when he moved to wilder quarters in the East Village at 441 E. 9th St. This apartment was up the street from the Cedar Tavern, where he went most every day or night. Recently a plaque was placed on the building at 441 to commemorate his residence.

Today the Cedar Tavern is located at 82 University Place. (We discuss the Cedar at greater length when you get to its original location at 24 University Place.) In the 1950s the Cedar had a rather bare interior. Now it's a charming bar with softly lit booths for quiet conversation. Nothing reminds you of its former history except the name—it was much less genteel in the days it was inhabited by Beat poets and Abstract Expressionist painters whose conversations weren't so quiet.

Walk south on University Place and stop at E. 10th St. in front of The Albert, 23 E. 10th St.

2   Thomas Wolfe

Thomas Wolfe.
Culver Pictures.

It's hard to realize how much influence Thomas Wolfe's novels had on young writers in America during the 1930s. Wolfe's *Look Homeward, Angel* brought to life a sweeping vision of pre-World War II America as seen from the window of a train traveling across the dark landscape. Lawrence Ferlinghetti has written that Kerouac's vision of America is like Wolfe's except that it is seen from a speeding car. And there is much more to *Look Homeward,*

Angel than that. It is the story of what Wolfe called "our buried life," and its hero Eugene Gant is a direct precursor to Kerouac in *The Town and the City*. Ferlinghetti and Seymour Krim attended the University of North Carolina, Chapel Hill, in part because Wolfe went there. Ferlinghetti's first writing was published in the student literary magazine that Wolfe had written for. One of the reasons Kerouac was attracted to New York in the first place was because Wolfe had lived there a long time, and he wanted to walk the same old streets. In an essay for a course at the New School in 1949 he said *Of Time and the River* is "one of the few big endeavors in 20th Century American writing to arrive at the divine secrets of solemn existence."

Wolfe taught at New York University in the Brown Building a few blocks away and lived in several places near the campus. From 1923 through 1925 he lived here at the Hotel Albert in room 2220. The six-story co-op apartment building is now refurbished as The Albert. (Perhaps if you stay there you can discover Wolfe's "unfound door.")

Continue south along University Place and stop between E. 9th and E. 8th St.

3   Hotel Lafayette

On the east side of University Place between E. 8th and E. 9th Streets was one of the finest small hotels in nineteenth-century New York, the Hotel Lafayette. The hotel has now been replaced by an apartment building naturally called The Lafayette. It was thoroughly French and attracted many returned expatriates and wannabee expatriates. Its café on the ground floor had the feeling of a true French café with marble-topped tables and wrought-iron chairs, now much-copied in chic uptown bistros. Lawrence Ferlinghetti stayed at the Hotel Lafayette during term breaks from the Sorbonne in the summers of 1948-1949. Kenneth Rexroth, another uncompromising anarchist poet with roots in San Francisco, stayed here with his parents when they went to New York on business trips in 1914 and 1915. These were exciting excursions for a Midwest boy. Rexroth's parents stayed at the Brevoort (one block west on Fifth Ave.) and the Lafayette, both then full of writers, artists, and journalists. He preferred the Lafayette because it was "the unrivaled meeting place of high bohemia." The Rexroths took along their nine-year-old Kenneth to the cafés and meeting places like Polly's Restaurant on MacDougal St. Emma Goldman was a habitué of Polly's, and Rexroth recalled hearing her defend her fellow anarchist and lover, Alexander Berkman, who in 1892 tried to assassinate industrialist Henry Clay Frick during the Homestead Strike against Carnegie Steel in Pittsburgh. (He didn't succeed, but his an-archism lived on in many poets like Rexroth.)

Directly across University Place on the west side of the street between E. 8th and E. 9th is the site of the old Cedar Street Tavern.

4   Cedar Street Tavern

The Cedar Street Tavern stood here at 24 University Place before the present high-rise luxury apartment went up. This was *the* artist's bar in New York during the 1950s. It was a home to all the Abstract Expressionists from Jackson Pollock to Willem de Kooning. The bar was plain, had no TV, no jukebox, just sturdy tables and booths. And they needed to be sturdy. The artists and their poet friends sometimes came to blows.

At one point Kerouac was barred from the Cedar Tavern for urinating into an ashtray or a sink (depending on conflicting ac-counts). Jackson Pollock was banned around the same time for kicking in the men's room door. It was also here that Kerouac met artist Stanley Twardowicz who became his closest buddy when he moved to Northport, Long Island.

Among the artists here were John Chamberlain, Willem de Kooning, Franz Kline, Al Leslie, Jackson Pollock, Larry Rivers (who painted the Cedar's menu on the wall), Mark Rothko, and David Smith. About the only painter who didn't frequent the bar was Lee Krassner, Pollock's wife, who avoided it because of all the fighting. Among the writers were John Ashbery, Gregory Corso, Ginsberg, John Clellon Holmes, LeRoi Jones, Kerouac, and Frank O'Hara who was a bridge between the painters and the poets. He worked at the Museum of Modern Art, wrote art criticism, and shone in both the literary and art worlds. On March 30, 1963, a large closing party was held at the Cedar. Then it was torn down to make way for the Brevoort East building that now dominates the entire block.

Turn the corner, walk west across 8th St., and stop just before reaching Fifth Ave.

5   Thomas Wolfe

In 1925 Thomas Wolfe moved into an apartment at 13 E. 8th St., sharing rent with Aline Bernstein, a stage designer. They had a large bare loft without plumbing and very little furniture. The walls were covered with Bernstein's theatrical sketches and the floor littered with Wolfe's manuscript pages. Here he began work on *Look Homeward, Angel,* and he described this house in a later book, *The Web and the Rock.* In the 1950s the building was torn down, but it's one of the sites Kerouac would have sought out in

Wolfe's New York.

Continue walking west on 8th St. and stop on the other side of
Fifth Ave. in front of the tall, eight-story brick building at No. 5.

6 Marlton Hotel

At 5 W. 8th St. just west of Fifth Ave. was a cheap, seedy hotel
called the Marlton. It's still here: Look for the name in stone above
the doorway. Jay Landesman stayed in this hotel on his first trip to
New York from St. Louis to promote his magazine, *Neurotica,* one
of the earliest avant-garde magazines to feature work by John
Clellon Holmes, Carl Solomon, and Allen Ginsberg.

Kerouac sometimes stayed here, as when Helen Weaver kicked
him out of her apartment for the last time. Her analyst agreed that
having Kerouac live with her had been a bad idea for her sanity. Of
that move Kerouac wrote in *Desolation Angels* : "the next day I get
a room in the Marlton Hotel on 8th Street and start typing what I
wrote in Mexico, double space neatly for the publishers." This
book was *Tristessa,* his story of a very *triste* love affair in Mexico.

Comedian Lenny Bruce also stayed here during his famous obscenity trial. As he remembered it, "in 1964, I got busted for obscenity at the Café Au Go Go. I continued performing and got
busted there again that same week." (Bruce was victimized by a
repressive society, but he also victimized himself; he should have
been called a stand-up tragedian.)

Walk west on 8th St. to MacDougal and stop at No. 32 W. 8th on
the southeast corner.

7 Eighth Street Bookshop

32 W. 8th St.
Photo by Bill Morgan.

The Eighth Street Bookshop at 32 W. 8th St. was the most vital bookstore in Manhattan for Beat literature. Here in the old, three-story brick building on the corner of MacDougal, Ted and Eli Wilentz opened the quintessential bookstore in 1947. Not content to run just a book shop, they began publishing books under the imprint of Corinth Books. Later they teamed up with LeRoi Jones of Totem books and published a series of ten seminal books of poetry by Kerouac, Ginsberg, Gary Snyder, and others.

When Ginsberg returned from India in early 1964, he stayed above the store with Ted Wilentz while looking for a place of his own. Al Aronowitz, a *New York Post* columnist who had written the first articles on the Beats, stopped by here to introduce Ginsberg to a young unknown folk singer, Bob Dylan. Wilentz had parties for Donald Allen, Ray Bremser, Ginsberg, Lawrence Ferlinghetti, LeRoi Jones, Jack Micheline, and activist David McReynolds. Among the poets the Wilentz brothers hired were John Wieners who worked here in 1962 and 1963 before moving to Boston and Hettie Jones who slaved in the office over the store. In February 1965 the bookstore moved across the street to 17 W. 8th and continued to operate there until the Wilentz' retired in the 1980s. (Cut-rate chain bookstores were encroaching on their territory, and they saw the cut-throat writing on the wall.)
Walk a little further west on 8th St. to No. 52.

8   Electric Lady Studios

These studios were in the basement of the 8th Street Playhouse at 52 W. 8th St. The recording studio was built by Jimi Hendrix in June 1969 at a cost of over one million dollars. An underground stream, Minetta Creek, delayed the construction. Although Hendrix left America for the last time on the day the studio opened, many others used it. Stevie Wonder recorded his *Talking Book* album here and the Rolling Stones and Billy Idol also cut records. In 1982, The Clash asked Allen Ginsberg to work with them on their *Combat Rock.* The building is vacant at present. A poster of Hendrix remains in a second-floor window, but who knows where the Electric Lady went?
Turn right at Sixth Ave. and turn right again onto W. 9th St. Stop at No. 58.

9   Dr. Perrone

In 1955, Kerouac went to court to contest his ex-wife Joan Haverty's suit for child support. Ever since Jan Kerouac's birth in 1952, Joan had been actively seeking child support from him. Ginsberg suggested he go to Dr. E. Perrone here at 58 W. 9th St. for the medical examinations to prove he couldn't work because of his severe phlebitis. Kerouac was prepared to take medical tests to disprove his paternity, even though in a letter to Ginsberg he confessed, "the dotter who I think looks like me, especially frowning square-browed photo, so may be mine." Eugene Brooks, Ginsberg's brother, was Kerouac's lawyer. Persuaded by Dr. Perrone's statements, the court held that Kerouac couldn't hold a job. Thus he evaded paying child support, and for years acted as if Jan Kerouac was not his daughter.

Return to Sixth Ave. and turn right to Balducci's Market near the corner.

10 Goody's Bar

Small shops with apartments above them once stood on the block now occupied by Balducci's gourmet store at 9th St. Here was Goody's Bar at 426 Sixth Ave. It had the longest bar in the Village until it closed in 1958. Kerouac arranged at least one press interview at Goody's Bar. (He talked better when he drank, he drank more when he talked.)

Cross Sixth Ave. and walk a block south to the pedestrian island between W. 8th and W. 9th St. You'll notice the beautiful Jefferson Market Branch of the New York Public Library. Built in 1877 as a courthouse, it's one of the finest examples of Victorian Gothic in the city.

11 Women's House of Detention

From the pedestrian island here you can get an overview of several of the sites on this tour. On the corner by the Jefferson Market Library is a beautiful garden that masks its earlier history as site of the Women's House of Detention. Until the mid-1950s this was where all female prisoners were kept while awaiting trial. Among the famous guests of the city have been Judith Malina of the Living Theatre, Dorothy Day of *The Catholic Worker*, and Angela Davis, former Weatherman activist and now professor at the University of California, Santa Cruz.

Allen Ginsberg was photographed here at a rally to legalize marijuana, standing in the snow, wearing a sign, "Pot is a reality trip." The photo made a popular poster in the late 1960s. This is also where Jerome Yulsman took the photograph of Jack Kerouac on the cover of Dennis McNally's book *Desolate Angel: A Biography* .

Look across Greenwich Ave. to the south side of the street. This is the next site on the tour.

12   Howard Johnson's

In early 1957 Ginsberg fixed up Kerouac on a blind date with
Joyce Glassman, a Barnard graduate just beginning her publishing
career. They agreed to meet at Howard Johnson's at 415 Sixth Ave.
and W. 8th St., where she bought him frankfurters, home fries,
and baked beans. He was broke, having just been short-changed
of his last $10. She described the scene in her book, *Minor Charac-
ters*. "He's the only person in Howard Johnson's in color," seeing
Kerouac's red-checked flannel lumberjack shirt. His own first im-
pressions: "It was the beginning of perhaps the best love affair I
ever had because Alyce [Joyce] was an interesting young person, a
Jewess, elegant middleclass sad and looking for something."
*The next site can also be seen on the other side of Sixth Ave.
where Sam Goody's is now.*

13   Waldorf Cafeteria

The Waldorf Cafeteria was an inexpensive restaurant where Allen
Ginsberg, e.e. cummings, Judith Malina, W.H. Auden, Jackson Pollock, Franz Kline, and Hans Hofmann went during the 1940s and
1950s to talk over cups of watery coffee. Diane di Prima wrote
about the Waldorf and so did Kerouac. In *Visions of Cody* he gives
a two-page description of the cafeteria and street scene, everything reflected in the front window, including the sign "Vegetarian
Plate 60¢." Joyce Johnson describes the Waldorf in *Minor Characters* as " . . . a uniform grey-brown. It had none of the chrome-
and-brass art-deco fittings of the Automat."
*Walk south on Sixth Ave. and turn left at Waverly Place. Almost
at the corner of the park is the Washington Square Hotel.*

14   Hotel Earle

When Bob Dylan came to New York from the Midwest in 1961 he
roosted briefly at the Hotel Earle at 103 Waverly Place. Now the
building has been renovated as the Washington Square Hotel. This
is an old 1902 stone and red brick building, and the three-story annex was added in 1916. At the time Dylan lived here it had a sad
run-down look. It wasn't long before he made it to grander lodgings.
*Walk east along Waverly Place and enter the park around the
Washington Arch.*

15   Washington Square/New York University (NYU)

Washington Square is still the beating heart of Greenwich Village.
Until the 1950s, traffic still ran through the arch and connected
lower Fifth Ave. with what is now LaGuardia Place (then called
West Broadway). The fight to ban traffic in the park was the first

major civic battle (1959) won by the *Village Voice*. Sundays, people from all over the city still come here to hang out, meet friends, listen to street musicians and soapbox orators, play chess, sit in the sun around the fountain, and witness one of the greatest natural human carnivals in the world (a far cry from the artificial malls of America).

In Ginsberg's "Howl" we read of those "who talked continuously seventy hours from park to pad to bar to Bellevue to museum to the Brooklyn Bridge," and no doubt the park was Washington Square, for the lives of the Beats crossed and recrossed the park continually, as every generation has.

A camera-eye focused on the park over the years might have recorded poet William Morris in a beatnik sailor suit getting busted for reading poetry without a permit, Allen Ginsberg reading the next week without getting busted, and Mary Travers of the future Peter, Paul and Mary singing folksongs by the fountain.

Allen Ginsberg in Washington Square Park.
Photo by Kaoru Sekine.

In June of 1952, Judith Malina and Julian Beck sat up all night at one of the chess tables on the southwest corner of the Square, translating *King Ubu* by Alfred Jarry. The Living Theatre's protests against taking shelter during A-bomb drills began in this park in the 1950s, as did countless other political demonstrations, protest poetry readings, and high camp and low camp spectacles of all kinds.

In 1950 *Neurotica* editor Jay Landesman met his future wife Fran Deitsch in Washington Square. They wrote *The Nervous Set,* a popular Broadway play of 1959, depicting their New York Bohemian lives, with a character based on Kerouac, played by unknown actor, Larry Hagman. It was the first and only play of the era to focus on the Beat-lifestyle in 1950s New York.

Album cover for The Nervous Set.
Courtesy of Columbia Records.

Exit Washington Square on the south side of the fountain and stop near the large, red sandstone library building at the corner of LaGuardia Place.

16   Bobst Library/Open Door

The main library at NYU is the massive building built in 1973 on the southeast corner of Washington Square. NYU's Rare Book and Manuscript collection, called the Fales Library, houses a significant collection of Beat literature, including the manuscript of Ginsberg's great "Kaddish."

Go one block south on LaGuardia Place to the corner of 3rd St.

The Bobst Library covers the site of the old Open Door on the northeast corner of LaGuardia Place and W. 3rd St. The Open Door was a tremendous barn-like jazz hang-out, where geniuses like Charlie Parker often blew the hot breath of their lives into their instruments. Performances cost a dollar and the Open Door booked the hippest groups, with late-night jam sessions after the musicians finished their regular gigs uptown on 52nd St. In *The Subterraneans* Kerouac calls it the Red Door, where "a wild generation party all smoky and mad . . . all sitting together, interesting groups at various tables . . . and up on the stand Bird Parker with solemn eyes."

Gregory Corso described a night here in his poem "For Miles" [Davis]: " . . . can you recall that 54 night at the Open Door / when you & bird / wailed five in the morning some wondrous / yet unimaginable score?"

Turn right on W. 3rd St. and walk west two blocks. Opposite the Fire Department is a building in which

Charlie Parker.
Photo by Bob Parent.

Edgar Allen Poe lived and breathed at No. 85 when this was known as Amity Street. Stop in the next block just past Sullivan St.

17 Café Caravan/Café Bizarre

For a time this section of E. 3rd St. rivaled MacDougal St. in the proliferation of coffee houses. The Café Caravan at 102 W. 3rd St. was a hot spot for poetry readings. It was the only building not torn down by NYU when they erected the new dorm on the south side of this block, but it's now a green grocer. Every Sunday night at 9:00 pm in the late 1950s the Caravan had an evening of poetry with Village poets like Ted Joans, William Morris, and Hugh Romney (later known to Woodstock fans as Wavy Gravy).

The Café Bizarre, owned by Rick Allman at 106 W. 3rd St., was one of the most crowded coffeehouses in the late 1950s. After reading *On the Road* at the age of sixteen, Janine Pommy Vega left home in New Jersey and got a summer job here. After high school, she returned to the Village and got to know Ginsberg, Herbert Huncke, Peter Orlovsky, and Ray and Bonnie Bremser. Janine married the Peruvian painter, Fernando Vega, and after his tragic death she wrote *Poems to Fernando,* published by City Lights Books in 1968. New York University tore down the entire block in the 1980s for the new law school dorm, Filomen D'Agostino Hall. *Turn right on MacDougal St., pass the Provincetown Playhouse made most famous by Eugene O'Neill's work, and turn left onto W. 4th St. Stop at the Washington Square Restaurant at the end of the block.*

18 Pony Stable Inn

Gregory Corso told Ginsberg that he was just out of prison for taking part in a robbery of a Household Finance office when they first met in a lesbian bar called the Pony Stable Inn (now the Washington Square Restaurant) at 150 W. 4th St. sometime around 1950. Like many of Corso's stories, this one about his crime was apocryphal. Corso showed his poems to Ginsberg who was greatly impressed. Corso told Ginsberg he had been watching a neighbor

Gregory Corso and Allen Ginsberg in photo booth.
©Allen Ginsberg Trust. Courtesy of Fahey/Klein Gallery, Los Angeles.

make love in the building across the street from his apartment window, and it turned out to be Allen himself and a girlfriend. *Stop at the corner of Sixth Ave. and W. 4th St. and look at the tall, wedge-shaped building across Sixth Ave.*

19   New Directions Publishing Co.

For many years New Directions Publishers, founded by James Laughlin, was headquartered in the tower-like building at 333 Sixth Ave. In the 1930s, Laughlin traveled much in Europe, visiting both Gertrude Stein and Ezra Pound. Pound told him, "you're never going to be a writer. Why don't you go back home to the States and do something useful?" He took Pound's advice and in 1936 returned home to found New Directions. Over the years the house has published much of the best avant-garde writing in the United States, presented the most important European writers in translation, and kept modern classics in print. New Directions is the publisher of William Carlos Williams, Herman Hesse, Franz Kafka, Ezra Pound, Dylan Thomas, Djuna Barnes, Kenneth Rexroth, Kenneth Patchen, Tennessee Williams, to name just a few.

During the late 1950s New Directions began publishing Beats and poets associated with the Beats, including Lawrence Ferlinghetti, Denise Levertov, Gregory Corso, Michael McClure, and Gary Snyder. "This was the tower of glory as far as I was concerned," Ferlinghetti recalled. "New Directions was publishing Ezra Pound and Dylan Thomas and all the greats of the American avant-garde. I was reading Patchen and Pound and Dylan Thomas then, and they were an enormous influence on me. These were the great early days of New Directions. Laughlin published books no one else would touch in his New Classics series." New Directions continues to be a courageous independent publisher, now at 80 8th Ave.

Go down Sixth Ave. two blocks and stop at the Locker Room sportswear store at No. 305.

20   Fugazzi Bar & Grill

Besides the San Remo, Fugazzi's at 305 Sixth Ave. was the most important hangout for the characters in Kerouac's *The Subterraneans*. (Kerouac renamed it Dante's in the novel.) Fugazzi's was located in the small space where the Locker Room store is now. In *The Subterraneans* the pushcart episode began in Fugazzi's with characters representing Kerouac, Gregory Corso, Stanley Gould, and Alene Lee. This episode was based on a drunken evening when Kerouac, Corso, and Lee stole a vegetable peddler's pushcart from Washington Square and took turns wheeling each other around town. Later they ended the evening at Ginsberg's apartment where arguments developed and Corso left with Kerouac's girlfriend. "Beginning, as I say with the pushcart incident — the night we drank red wine at Dante's and were in a drinking mood now both of us so disgusted . . . " This pivotal moment in the story foretold the split between the main characters.

This bar also figured in a line in Ginsberg's "Howl" describing people "Who sank all night in submarine light of Bickford's floated out and sat through the stale beer afternoon in desolate Fugazzi's, listening to the crack of doom on the hydrogen jukebox." In the annotated version of the poem, Ginsberg carefully explained that Bickford's was a cafeteria without a jukebox and he needed a location like Fugazzi's with a jukebox for his narrative. *Directly across the street from the Locker Room is a tiny street called Minetta Lane. Walk halfway up Minetta Lane and you'll see that there is an even tinier street intersecting it called Minetta Street. Stop at the quiet intersection to read about the next site.*

21 Romero's/The Fat Black Pussycat

The Fat Black Pussycat.
Photo by Bill Morgan.

At the end of 1956 in a letter to John Clellon Holmes, Kerouac described Romero's at 24 Minetta Lane (where La Bohème is today) as the greatest new bar in the Village. Poet Fielding Dawson wrote: "The jukebox was to the left of the door, and beyond it was a small rectangular wooden table, which fit into a small corner, fitted with an L-shaped bench, and beyond that on the left still, were a lot of posters most of Negro guys and women . . . the bar ran the length of the place, opposite the jukebox." In the summer a small garden was open out back with three or four tables. Guidebooks describe it as a "racially mixed scene" run by Johnny Romero, a

West Indian, with a calypso jukebox.

The painted sign for The Fat Black Pussycat is still visible on the brick wall at 13 Minetta St. A café and club in the 1950s and 1960s, today it's a Mexican restaurant. Here in the early 1960s the media discovered a campy singing waiter with a terrible voice. He became famous as Tiny Tim. (While you're here take a look at No. 7 on the left just past the restaurant. This was the home of the policeman, Frank Serpico, who exposed widespread corruption in the New York Police Department and on whom the movie *Serpico*, starring Al Pacino, was based.)

You can exit Minetta St. just past Serpico's house and turn right back on Sixth Ave. Return north on Sixth Ave. for two blocks to 3rd St. and turn right; you won't be able to miss the McDonald's playground at the corner. Stop at No. 147.

22   Eddie Condon's/Tony Pastor's

In the mid-1950s this short section of W. 3rd St. between Sixth Ave. and LaGuardia Place was truly Night Club Row. Eddie Condon's, a crowded jazz and Dixieland club, was at 147 W. 3rd St. In the red brick building at 130 W. 3rd St., where the new Kettle of Fish now operates, was Tony Pastor's. One night in May 1955 Kerouac went there attracted by the belly dancing. He wrote to Burroughs that he had watched the dancers and sailors and felt he was one of the "sexless American heroes" described in *Junky*.

Continue east on 3rd St., turn right at the corner of MacDougal, and stop at the Café Reggio.

23   Café Reggio/Café Wha?

The Café Reggio at 121 MacDougal St. is one of the only survivors from the era of the bohemian coffeehouse, doing nonstop business since 1927. Bob Dylan's first New York performance in the early 1960s was at the Café Wha? (now located at 115 MacDougal St. on the corner of Minetta Lane). You can still listen to live rock'n'roll, rhythm and blues, and Motown tunes here. Look overhead for the Players Theater sign, one of the many off-off-Broadway theaters housed in this building over the years. In the 1950s the Gene Frankel Repertory Theater did many experimental pieces here, some successful, others not. (This theater is still going strong at another location in the Village off Lafayette St.)

Continue south on MacDougal St. This was the center of Village nightlife during the 1950s and 1960s . Stop at No. 113 MacDougal.

24   Minetta Tavern/Rienzi Coffeehouse

One of the last vestiges of the old Italian neighborhood that once flourished here is the Minetta Tavern on the corner. For a while it was a speakeasy where Ernest Hemingway or John Dos Passos might be found. The most famous character of the Minetta Tavern was Joe Gould, sometimes called Professor Seagull, for his habit of cawing like a gull. He was reported for decades to be compil-

Minetta Tavern.
Photo by Bill Morgan.

ing a book entitled *The Oral History of the World*. When he died in 1957 at the age of 68, the famed Village street philosopher's work was found not to be so extensive. It was mostly written on the wind that blows between bar stools. Gould himself was the subject of an e.e. cummings poem that begins "little joe gould has lost his teeth and doesn't know where to find them . . . ."

In the 1940s, Ginsberg and Lucien Carr had unrecorded conversations here. They remember writing graffiti on the men's room walls. Kerouac wrote in *Visions of Duluoz* that "Burroughs bought us fine dinners, in Romey Marie's, in San Remo's, in Minetta's, and inevitably Kammerer would always find us and join in." Minetta's drew the same "subterranean" patrons as the San Remo down the block. The floor was covered with sawdust and the walls with caricatures, some done by artists like Franz Kline, in exchange for drinks.

The Minetta was on Gregory Corso's home turf, and here in 1951 Corso got into a hassle over Marisol Escobar, the artist he was dating. Corso smashed a glass in his rival's face and cut his own hand.

Across the street on the east side of the block, look for No. 116.

25   Gas Light Café/Kettle of Fish

One coffeehouse that made this area a center of bohemian life in the 1960s was the Gas Light Café, in the basement of 116 MacDougal St. Originally a gay bar in the 1940s, the MacDougal Street Bar's owner John Mitchell turned it into the quintessential Beat hangout. Mike Wallace even did television interviews with Beats here on May 15, 1960.

In the late 1950s, the Gas Light was the first café with poetry readings in the Village. The practice spread to other coffee houses. Readers included Ray Bremser, Gregory Corso, Diane di Prima, Lawrence Ferlinghetti, Allen Ginsberg, LeRoi Jones, Kerouac, Jack Micheline, and Peter Orlovsky. A few issues of the *Gaslight Poetry Review* were also published here, much to everyone's flickering illumination.

POETRY READING

allen ginsberg
gregory corso
ray bremser

Sunday, Feb. 15, 1959 at 4 P.M.

THE GASLIGHT
116 mac dougal street
greenwich village

Poster courtesy of Allen Ginsberg Archive, Stanford University.

Kerouac's friend, Henri Cru, lived on the top-floor apartment in the same building before moving to W. 13th St. in the 1960s, he introduced Kerouac to Edie Parker who became Jack's first wife. Kerouac described Henri as "that fantastic character I lived with on the West Coast in my road days, who stole everything in sight but gave it away to widows sometimes (Bon coeur, good heart) and who was now living meanly I'd say in an apartment on 13th Street near the waterfront with an icebox (in which nevertheless he still stored his home made special recipe chicken consomme)."

Next door at 114 MacDougal St. was the Kettle of Fish, the most popular of the hip bars. Allen Ginsberg, Gregory Corso, Bob Dylan, Edie Sedgwick, and Andy Warhol often stewed in this kettle. The photograph of Kerouac with Joyce Johnson, on the dust jacket of her *Minor Characters* was taken in front. In the 1990s, The Gap used the same photo in an ad for khakis, but airbrushed Joyce Johnson out, leaving a gap in the truth.
Continue on MacDougal south to Bleecker St.

26   San Remo

On the northwest corner of MacDougal and Bleecker St. at 93 MacDougal, the San Remo, now called Carpo's Cafe, was a famous Bohemian coffeehouse of the 1940s and 1950s. It had wooden booths, black-and-white tile floors, and a pressed-tin ceiling, all of which are gone now.

In *The Subterraneans* Kerouac placed the San Remo in San Francisco and renamed it the Mask. But all the events in the book took place here in New York. Ginsberg coined the term "subterraneans" to describe the alienated, the disaffected, and the bohemians who hung out in places like the San Remo. It first opened in 1923 in what

was then a predominantly Italian neighborhood. Under the owner-
ship of Joe Santini, it remained a hangout for hipsters, writers, and
artists well into the 1950s. In *Down and In: Life in the Underground,*
Ron Sukenick called it "an actual Village-Bohemian-literary-artis-
tic-underground-mafioso-pinko-revolutionary-subversive-intellec-
tual-existentialist-anti-bourgeois café." Carl Solomon first took
Ginsberg to the San Remo in 1948 to meet Philip Lamantia, a San
Francisco poet who had dropped out of high school to join the
French Surrealists-in-exile in New York. Ginsberg shortly thereafter
brought Kerouac to the Remo, where he began creating the charac-
ters who would populate the pages of *The Subterraneans.* The list is
long of those who hung at the San Remo: Alan Ansen, William
Gaddis, Stanley Gould, Bill Keck, Alene Lee, Anton Rosenberg, Gore
Vidal, James Agee, Julian Beck, Chandler Brossard, Anatole Broyard,
William Burroughs, John Cage, Gregory Corso, Merce Cunningham,
Miles Davis, Paul Goodman, John Clellon Holmes, Chester Kallman,
Kenneth Koch, Judith Malina, Harold Norse, Frank O'Hara, Jackson
Pollock, Larry Rivers, James Schuyler, and Tennessee Williams.

Judith Malina says that the idea of the Living Theatre was born
at the San Remo. The writer Maxwell Bodenheim, a village character but also a colorful writer, hung out here cadging drinks. He
said Greenwich Village was "the Coney Island of the soul." Chandler Brossard called the San Remo in his 1952 book, *Who Walk in
Darkness,* "a divine and exclusive retreat." The New York crime
photographer Weegee came here nightly, and who knows what
dastardly crimes he might have captured.

Here Ginsberg had a chance encounter with the great Welsh
poet, Dylan Thomas. Thomas came into the San Remo quite
loaded one night and struck up a conversation. He said he'd just
been offered "sex for money" by a young woman on the street, and
he asked Ginsberg with a straight face, "Do you know any ama-
teurs?" Later Ginsberg tried, unsuccessfully, to impress him poeti-
cally, the way young poets later tried to impress Ginsberg with
their own literary genius.

Ginsberg said the San Remo was "a center of Kerouac's N.Y. social
life." One drunken night Kerouac met Gore Vidal here and went home
with him. A couple of times Kerouac was beaten up outside the bar.
"I've been getting sillydrunk again lately in Remo . . ." Kerouac said in
1954. In *The Subterraneans* Kerouac wrote," . . . going then to the
Mask [San Remo] as usual, beers, get worse drunk, then out to walk
home." On the way home, he, Corso, and Alene Lee stole a pushcart,
and left it at Ginsberg's apartment, causing some havoc.
Directly across Bleecker St. from the San Remo is No. 190.

27 Gregory Corso

Gregory Corso was born in 1930 in nearby St. Vincent's Hospital and was brought home to 190 Bleecker St. (above today's Fantastic Ray's Pizza). He observes the apartment in his poem "Birthplace Revisited": "I stand in the dark light in the dark street / and look up at my window, I was born there. / The lights are on; other people are moving about."

Kerouac wrote in a preface to Corso's *Gasoline:* "Gregory was a tough young kid from the lower East Side who rose like an angel over the rooftops and sang Italian songs as sweet as Caruso and Sinatra, but in *words.*"

In Little Italy, Corso's mother disappeared when he was an infant, and his father dropped his children in foster homes. He got into a lot of trouble and did time in reform schools and orphanages, but educated himself in public libraries. He went to jail for stealing a suit when he was sixteen or seventeen. In Dannemora Prison he continued his self-education, a voracious reader especially of poetry such as Shelley's.

The next stop is on the southeast corner of Bleecker and MacDougal St.

28 Café Figaro

At 186 Bleecker St. is the Café Figaro, formerly called The Borgia and The Scene. The original Figaro opened in January 1956 at 195 Bleecker St. Owner John Mitchell served espresso from noon to 1 A.M., and the European-style café became popular with the hip Village crowd in the late 1950s. In the mid-1950s the *Village Voice* wrote that the Figaro "lacks sympathy for Beats," but at one time the café had a mural of "beatniks," and plenty of poets and wannabees hung out here.

Go south on MacDougal St. and stop at No. 92-94.

29 Bob Dylan

Bob Dylan continued to live in the Village after he made it big, but on a grander scale. In 1966 he bought two adjoining townhouses and made one large house here at 92-94 MacDougal St. These houses were part of the MacDougal-Sullivan Gardens built in the 19th century. There's a sign on the street in front of Dylan's house giving the history of the block. Before his horrific motorcycle accident and his move to Woodstock in 1968, Dylan recorded "Blonde On Blonde" and other early songs while living here. The communal backyard gardens can be seen from the rear windows of the Pizza Box restaurant around the corner on Bleecker St.

Bob Dylan's townhouse.
Photo by Bill Morgan.

Return to Bleecker St. and turn right to The Atrium at No. 160.

30 Mills House and The Village Gate

In 1951 Allen Ginsberg lived in a flophouse known as the Mills House at 160 Bleecker St. He paid $2 a night. Built in 1896 as a hostel for poor gents, the building had 1,500 tiny rooms. It's now been converted into a fancy apartment building called The Atrium, but you can still make out the name "Mills House" high up on the pediment over the front door.

Art D'Lugoff, a big music promoter in the city, negotiated a 48-year lease here for a basement space, in which he opened the Village Gate in 1958. Originally the entrance was around the corner at 185 Thompson St., but was later moved to Bleecker St. All the jazz greats like Gillespie, Miles, Mingus, Monk, and Odetta worked and played here.

In 1980 D'Lugoff held a Beat weekend reunion with Ginsberg, Amiri Baraka, Ray Bremser, Herbert Huncke, Jack Micheline, Peter Orlovsky, and the Fugs. Playwright and actor, Sam Shepard, worked here as a waiter when he first came to New York in 1963 and must have mumbled some dramatic asides. The Village Gate closed in the early 1990s after

Mills House.
Photo by Bill Morgan.

thirty years of history-making sound. The premises are still echoing.

Continue east on Bleecker St. and stop in the next block between Thompson St. and LaGuardia Place.

31   Bleecker Street Music Strip/Bitter End

Although some of the names of the music joints along Bleecker St. between Sullivan St. and LaGuardia Place have changed a dozen times in the past thirty years, the street still has the same jumping Saturday-night vibes it always had. A few of the stars who have played on the strip are: Joan Baez, Jimi Hendrix, Buddy Holly, Janis Joplin, The Mamas and the Papas, Jim Morrison and the Doors, Phil Ochs, Simon and Garfunkel, Patti Smith, Steppenwolf, The Velvet Underground, and Frank Zappa and the Mothers of Invention. Another famous club, the Bitter End at 147 Bleecker St, still exists. Woody Allen, George Carlin, Bill Cosby, Bob Dylan, Peter, Paul and Mary, Richard Pryor, and Carly Simon all appeared here, took their bows, and went on down the tunnel of time.

On the south side of the street in this same block stop in front of No. 152.

32   Café Au Go Go

In the basement at 152 Bleecker St. (now torn down) was the Café Au Go Go where Lenny Bruce was arrested on obscenity charges. And this is where a very young Bruce Springsteen made his first New York appearance in 1966 with his high school band, the Castilles. The Blues Project recorded at Au Go Go and Eric Clapton and Cream played here on their second U.S. trip late in 1967.

Return to Thompson St. and walk south to No. 180.

33   Frank Zappa

Frank Zappa, one of rock 'n' roll's most acute social critics, lived at 180 Thompson St. at the height of his fame in the late 1960s. While here he made four albums with his original group of eccentrics, The Mothers of Invention (who were very much zapped by Ed Sanders and Tuli Kupferberg's Fugs band). The albums were *Lumpy Gravy, We're Only In It for the Money, Uncle Meat,* and *Cruisin' With Ruben and the Jets.*

Go two blocks further south on Thompson St. and turn right on Prince St. to No. 181.

34   Carl Solomon/Anatole Broyard/Stanley Gould

In 1951 Carl Solomon and his wife, Olive, moved to this six-floor brick and stone building at 181 Prince St., a few blocks from the San Remo, where Solomon could often be found. In those days this was still Little Italy on the border of the warehouse district that is now soft-chic Soho. The Solomons' relationship did not thrive here, to put it mildly, and the next year they were divorced. Writer Anatole Broyard also lived here, subletting an apartment to Solomon. Broyard described the scene in his memoir *Kafka Was the Rage:* "It was a tenement . . . built for immigrants, old and shabby, a tiny top-floor walk-up divided into three little boxes like walk-in closets. It was cramped and dingy, but I didn't care." Around this time, when Carl and Olive Solomon, Ginsberg, John Clellon Holmes, and Stanley Gould were working for National Opinion Research, Solomon got a job with his uncle, A.A. Wyn, at Ace paperbacks. It was through this heavenly connection that Ace printed William Burroughs' first book, *Junky,* and contracted for Kerouac's *On the Road* (but didn't publish it; who knows why not).

Stanley Gould, who also lived at No. 181 above the Solomons, was Broyard's model for his essay "Portrait of a Hipster." Ronald Sukenick, author of *Down and In: Life in the Underground,* remembers that the building was full of weird Bohemians, one of whom "threw his bed out the window and painted his apartment black at the end of his marriage." "Wise as Solomon" was not a description Olive would have used . . .

Carl Solomon.
©Allen Ginsberg Trust. Courtesy of Fahey/Klein Gallery, Los Angeles.

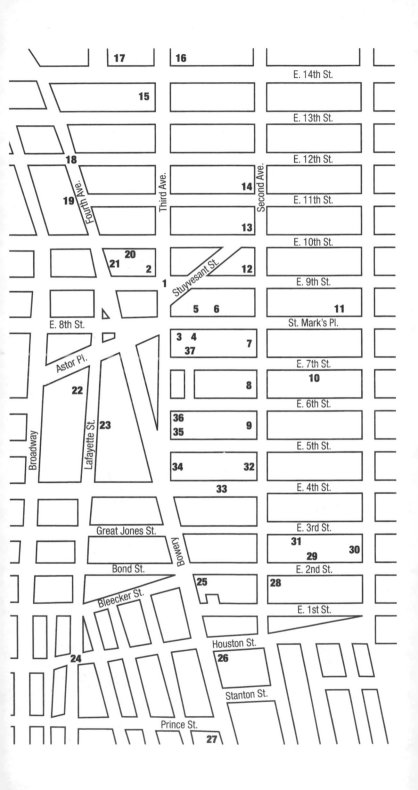

Lawrence Ferlinghetti in garden, 1961.
©Allen Ginsberg Trust. Courtesy of Fahey/Klein Gallery, Los Angeles.

East Village
Tour 1

Length of tour: 2 ½ hours
Subway: #6 to Astor Place
Bus: M1, 2, 3, 101, or 102 to St. Mark's Place/8th St.
Begin this tour at the corner of Third Ave. and E. 9th St.

1   Third Avenue El

Before subways were dug under the streets at the turn of the century, elevated train trestles were built for the first rapid transit systems. One was the Third Avenue El, a major feature of the landscape from 1878 until torn down in 1955-1956. For fifty years it dominated the street scene, making Third Ave. noisy, dark, and dirty, a fit atmosphere for the dingy bars Kerouac loved to inhabit.

When he heard of the removal of the El in early 1956 he sadly wrote Lucien Carr, "we've had our last drink under the last pillar of the 3rd Avenue El . . . "

The Third Avenue El appeared in Lawrence Ferlinghetti's *Pictures of the Gone World* in a poem he wrote on the train going to Columbia. The poem begins:

"Reading Yeats I do not think / of Ireland / but of midsummer New York / and of myself back then / reading that copy I found / on the Thirdavenue El / the El / with its flyhung fans / and its signs reading / SPITTING IS FORBIDDEN / the El / careening thru its thirdstory world /with its thirdstory people / in their thirdstory doors / looking as if they had never heard / of the ground . . . "

Imagine this street under the trestles of steel girders and dirty beams with an enormous station here at 9th St. Stan Brakhage filmed the El in 1955 at the suggestion of Joseph Cornell who thought the passing of an era should be documented before the El was torn down. Brakhage's film was called *The Wonder Ring*. Cornell later used the footage in his own film *GNIR Rednow*. **Look across the street at the store on the northwest corner of Third Ave. and E. 9th St.**

2   Western Music Company

At 34 Third Ave. once stood a building that housed the Western Music Company, described by Jack Kerouac in *Visions of Cody*. The 'beat' Central Employment Agency was located on the second floor of an ancient, three-story red brick building, now replaced by the monstrous white apartment house. Although the building is gone, you can learn more than you need to know by reading Kerouac's detailed description. Outside you'll see the same "dirty piss splashed and littered sooty sidewalk in front" that Kerouac did. Some things don't change, especially the sidewalks of New York, so often idealized in song.

In this building Robert Frank, the great Swiss photographer and filmmaker, lived in a loft with his wife Mary and their two children in the late 1950s. Kerouac and Joyce Johnson were irregular visitors. Kerouac liked Frank and wrote the introduction to his photo book *The Americans*. He said Frank knew "how to become a shadow." Kerouac imagined his job as a writer was similar; to see and report events without taking part or influencing them. In this loft they planned the 1959 movie *Pull My Daisy*, produced and directed by Robert Frank and Alfred Leslie and narrated by Kerouac. They were all great friends, although in the film it was never clear who pulled whose daisy.

Go south one block on Third Ave. to the corner of St. Mark's Place. You'll see a pizza/bagel parlor on the corner. This was the Sagamore cafeteria. Across the street is Cooper Union, which has long been the intellectual heart of the area. Abraham Lincoln, Emma Goldman, Mark Twain, Susan B. Anthony, and many Beat writers and poets presented their trenchant or far-out visions here.

3   The Sagamore/Valencia Hotel/Five Spot

The Sagamore, an all-night cafeteria which stood at 19 Third Ave. on the southeast corner of St. Mark's Place, was much visited, and described by Kerouac as "the respectable bums' cafeteria." For Joyce Johnson it was "a cafeteria for the real poor. Nothing voluntary in the destitution of the bums and old people who are its main customers." One night in October 1952 after a concert at Cooper Union, John Cage, Merce Cunningham, Piero Heliczer, Harold Norse, Julian Beck, and Judith Malina came here to celebrate, and there were many other all-night confabs.

The Sagamore was in the same building as the Valencia Hotel, now slightly refurbished as the St. Mark's Hotel, at 2 St. Mark's Place. James Grauerholz, secretary and companion to William S. Burroughs for twenty years, took a room in this fleabag hotel in 1973 when he arrived from Kansas. It was Grauerholz who suggested that Burroughs move to Lawrence, Kansas in 1981 to flee the distractions and dissipations of city life.

Also on the street level of this building is the last location of the Five Spot jazz bar, located around the corner near 4th St. (See site No. 34 ahead.)

Walk east on St. Mark's Place to No. 4, the Trash and Vaudeville store.

4   Bridge Theater

The dilapidated three-story red-brick building at 4 St. Mark's Place was once a fashionable nineteenth-century townhouse. Now it's a vintage clothing store. During the 1960s, the Bridge Theater was here, across the street from the Dom nightclub. The theater was a center for Happenings and the Fluxus art movement. Happenings, as con-

Site of the Bridge Theater.
Photo by Bill Morgan.

ceived by Allan Kaprow, were improvised multi-media events with dance, film, music, and audience participation (or alienation). The Bridge staged works by Kaprow as well as Claes Oldenburg, Robert Rauschenberg, Jim Dine, Red Grooms, Al Hansen, and the Bread and Puppet Theatre. The Fugs had a four-week standing-room-only run here in 1965. On one night, fans rushed the stage and tore the clothes off the performers and fugged-up their instruments.

Jonas Mekas was arrested at the Bridge Theater on obscenity charges for showing Jack Smith's *Flaming Creatures* and Jean Genet's *La Chant D'Amour* in 1965. At a performance here in April 1967 the U.S. flag was burned, and the city tried to revoke the theater's license. The New York Eternal Committee for Freedom of the Arts was formed, including Andy Warhol, Jonas Mekas, and Allen Ginsberg, who met with city officials. Mayor Lindsay promised to look into the matter, and the theater stayed open. In other less obscene incarnations, it has been the Little Theatre, the Tempo Playhouse, and the New Bowery Theatre. As the New Bowery in 1964 it staged one-act plays by Diane di Prima, Frank O'Hara, Wallace Stevens, and others who deserve to remain anonymous.

Look across the street at the building with the basement store called Religious Sex.

5   Carl Solomon

In the summer of 1950, Carl Solomon and his new wife, Olive Blake, moved to this ornately decorated building at 7 St. Mark's Place. Solomon, to whom Ginsberg's "Howl" is dedicated, was also the author of *Mishaps Perhaps* and *More Mishaps,* both published by City Lights Books, as well as *Emergency Messages* (Paragon House). The Solomons rented their apartment from painter Henry Sexton, and the mishaps began.

Walk a little farther east on St. Mark's Place to the large white and blue building on the north side of the street at Nos. 19-23.

6   The Dom

The large community center at 23 St. Mark's Place was once The Dom, a seminal trend-setting night club. In the early 1960s Stanley Tolkin, owner of Stanley's bar on Avenue B, moved to these larger quarters. Built at the turn of the century as Arlington Community Hall, it was a Polish club when Tolkin bought it. He brought with him his own house band, the poet/musicians known as The Fugs: Tuli Kupferberg, Ed Sanders, and Ken Weaver. Bringing together rock, radical comedy, and hilarious obscenity, they created an irreverent and politically conscious new musical form. They were mothers of the Mothers of Invention and other groups. Among the raucous and ribald songs in their six albums were "Slum Goddess," "Boobs A Lot," "Group Grope," and "Kill For Peace."

The popularity of The Dom accelerated in April 1966 when Andy Warhol and Paul Morrissey rented it for a series of performances. With a large dance floor, it was just the right space for Warhol's hip, young crowd. The Dom soon became *the* hangout for anyone under 25. Bar or not, no liquor was sold to the psychedelic crowd who came for the light shows; alcohol was not the drug of choice for the crowd who loved Warhol's newest discovery, The Velvet Underground, with Nico, Lou Reed, and John Cale. Everyone danced under strobe lights to booming music at The Dom, the father of disco. The slogan "A good club becomes its clientele" was never truer than here.

Later The Dom became The Electric Circus, with The Family Stone, The Mothers of Invention, and The Fugs. Bob Dylan named the hall above "The Balloon Farm," inspired by Warhol's inflated silver balloon sculptures. When a small bomb injured many people in March 1970, The Dom was doomed. It closed its doors for good in August 1971.

Go east along St. Mark's Place and stop at Second Ave. in front of the newsstand.

7 Gem Spa/B&H Dairy Restaurant

Gem Spa.
Photo by Bill Morgan.

The Gem Spa at 131 Second Ave. on the corner of St. Mark's Place is a neighborhood institution, the newspaper and magazine pickup point for East Village artists and writers. Allen Ginsberg mentions getting his paper here in "Rain-Wet Asphalt Heat, Garbage Curbed Cans Overflowing," and Ted Berrigan refers to the Gem Spa in several poems. Don McNeill of the *Village Voice* wrote in 1966 that "the sidewalk seems to run through the candy store. . . . By virtue of its location, twenty-four-hour vigil, and survival stock of tobacco, Bambu papers, and egg creams, it is the official oasis of the East Village."

Walk south on Second Ave. to the B&H Dairy Restaurant at No. 127.

This tiny diner is just as it was in the 1950s, one of the cheapest neighborhood restaurants. As Joyce Johnson tells the story in *Minor Characters,* she first meet Hettie Cohen Jones on the street-corner here passing out flyers for her husband LeRoi's poetry reading. LeRoi and Hettie warmed to each other over coffee in the B&H, and the heat lasted for years.

Continue south on Second Ave. to the southwest corner of 7th St.

8   Kiev Restaurant/Ratner's/Fillmore East

Robert Frank at the Kiev Restaurant, March 1984.
©Allen Ginsberg Trust. Courtesy of Fahey/Klein Gallery, Los Angeles.

Open since 1978, the Kiev Restaurant at 117 Second Ave. plays much the same role today as did Ratner's and Rappaport's restaurants in the 1950s and 1960s, a serious all-night eatery. Allen Ginsberg was a steady customer at the Kiev, and used it for back-drops in his photographic portraits of friends like Robert Frank, Philip Glass, and Francesco Clemente. Here it is in his 1986 poem "Hard Labor": " . . . I'm a fairy with purple wings and white halo / translucent as an onion ring in / the transsexual fluorescent light of Kiev / Restaurant after a hard day's work."

Continue south on Second Ave. to the block near the Met Supermarket.

Just down the street from the Kiev was the greatest of the all-night Kosher Delis of the 1950s, Ratner's. It was located at 111 Second Ave., where the Met Supermarket is today. This was the largest and the noisiest of the Second Ave. delis, with colorful patrons and irritable waiters serving blintz, kreplach, and stuffed cabbage. In the 1960s when Bill Graham's Fillmore East was next door, this deli overflowed with the theater crowd and with performers like the Grateful Dead. A ghostly Andy Warhol often ate here and was never the worse for it. Don McNeill said Warhol "looked pale under the lights." In Ted Berrigan's poem "Memorial Day" he refers to the death of the mother of Bernadette Mayer, an East Village poet:

"... Bernadette had to arrange her mother's funeral age 15 / & we're in Ratner's 3 AM . . ."

There is a Ratner's still in operation on Delancey St. near Essex, with the same menu, decor, and waiters who may moonlight elsewhere as character actors.

The theater next door to Ratner's at 105 Second Ave. had many lives and reincarnations until it was finally demolished in 1996. Only the facade remains of what was originally Loew's Commodore in 1928, an ornate movie palace. In the mid-1960s it became the Village Theatre with popular concerts such as the "Illumination of the Buddha Psychedelic Celebration #3" with Timothy Leary, Allen Ginsberg, and others. According to the *New York Times,* "Dr. Leary holds a substantial portion of his audience quivering in molecular ecstasy." Other performers: Chuck Berry, John Coltrane, and Buck Owens and the Buckaroos.

As the Fillmore East in the late 1960s, this theater flourished under rock promoter Bill Graham who booked all the great bands here and at his original Fillmore in San Francisco, after which this theater was named. Among the performers: The Doors, The Grateful Dead, Jimi Hendrix, The Jefferson Airplane with Grace Slick, and Janis Joplin with Big Brother and the Holding Company. The Who staged *Tommy* here for the first time in November 1969. This block of Second Ave. has been renamed Bill Graham's Way. The Fillmore East closed on June 27, 1971 and the theater then was used for occasional concerts until it was renovated as The Saint, a lavishly decorated gay dance club that lasted until May 2, 1988.
Continue south on Second Ave. to No. 93, between 6th and 5th St.

9   Rappaport's

Another of the many Kosher Jewish restaurants along Second Ave. was Rappaport's at 93 Second Ave., smaller and cozier than Ratner's. Both Rappaport's and Ratner's down the block were known for their surly waiters who were sometimes really lovable curmudgeons. This dairy restaurant had spectacular blintzes. Today it is a fashionable, hip restaurant called Global 33, where service is friendlier, but the prices have gone global.

Go back up Second Ave. and turn right on E. 7th St. Stop at No. 64 where the Style Lab is now located.

10   Les Deux Megots Coffeehouse

The basement/storefront of the old brick townhouse at 64 E. 7th St. was the important Les Deux Megots Coffeehouse, a much larger café than the tiny Tenth Street Coffee House also owned by Mickey Ruskin. In late 1962, when poetry readings at the café on Tenth Street became big, Ruskin moved here, where Monday and Wednesday night readings continued, organized by Paul Blackburn. Among the poets: Rochelle Owens, Jerome Rothenberg, and Blackburn himself. A literary magazine, *Poets at Les Deux Megots,* combined Beats and Black Mountain poets, Deep Image poets, and younger New York School poets. In the winter of 1963 readings were re-established at the Café Le Metro. In 1964 a macrobiotic restaurant here called the Paradox had readings hosted by Will Inman. Mickey Ruskin went on to open Max's Kansas City, perhaps the most notable downtown New York night spot of the late 1960s, which was to become Andy Warhol's private club.

Continue east on 7th St., turn left on First Ave. for one block, and then turn left again to 77 St. Mark's Place.

11   W.H. Auden

A plaque on the building at 77 St. Mark's Place marks W.H. Auden's life here from 1953 to 1972. Most of that time Auden shared the apartment with Chester Kallman. It was a floor-through apartment with a sleeping room off the living room, a separate study for Auden, and a large, cluttered kitchen where they had gourmet meals and memorable dinner parties for people like Ginsberg, Gregory Corso, Igor Stravinsky, Christopher Isherwood, and many foreign literati who brought fame to Auden's doorstep. David Jackson said the apartment was "a sad scene of sagging bookshelves, sprung-seat overstuffed chairs, a dusty and scarred 'cozy-corner' and everywhere litter, piles of paper and magazines, this morning's crusted dish of egg."

Stalkers are not something new in Manhattan. A woman followed Auden around for years while he was living here. Once she bribed the superintendent of the building to let her into his apartment where she measured his suit for a new one. She told people she was pregnant by Auden although they had met only once, and that was at a hearing when she was committed to a psychiatric ward. While here Auden wrote *City Without Walls* and *Epistle to a Godson.* He wrote the libretto for *Elegy for Young Lovers* in 1959 with Chester Kallman. Although Auden remained too British to ever be Beat, he had a certain gay affinity with some of the poets who lived in the Village.

Go west on St. Mark's Place to Second Ave. and turn right. One block north on the west side of the street is the Telephone Bar and Grill with bright red British phone booths in front.

12   Café Le Metro

In the 1960s, the Café Le Metro, owned by Moe and Cindy Margulies, was located at 149 Second Ave. where the Telephone Bar and Grill now stands. After Les Deux Megots Coffeehouse closed in February of 1963, many literary readings were held here. In February 1964, the Café Le Metro became the battleground for one of the more important First Amendment fights in the city's literary history. A city license inspector appeared at a reading by Jackson MacLow and issued a summons, citing the New York Coffee House Law of 1962, which outlawed unlicensed "entertainment." This would have put the small neighborhood coffeehouses that did not serve liquor out of business. Cabaret licenses were much too expensive, with more stringent fire department codes and other regulations. The poetry community led by Ginsberg, Paul Blackburn, and Ted Berrigan fought for and won the right to read poetry without a cabaret permit.

Poets Carol Bergé, Paul Blackburn, Allen Katzman, and Susan Sherman ran readings here on Monday and Wednesday nights and Sunday afternoons. Poets who spoke and sang at Le Metro were Julian Beck, Ted Berrigan, Paul Blackburn, William Burroughs, Gregory Corso, Diane di Prima, Bob Dylan, Lawrence Ferlinghetti, Allen Ginsberg, Herbert Huncke, LeRoi Jones, Denise Levertov, Gerard Malanga, Frank O'Hara, Peter Orlovsky, Charles Reznikoff, and John Wieners. One night after a reading, filmmaker Barbara Rubin took Ginsberg, Peter Orlovsky, Rose Pettet, Ed Sanders, and other poets to the new Dom around the corner and the East Village art crowd followed these cultural Pied Pipers.

Go north on Second Ave. to the corner of 10th St.

St. Mark's-in-the-Bouwerie.
Courtesy of the Poetry Project.

13 St. Mark's-in-the-Bouwerie

St. Mark's-in-the-Bouwerie, at the corner of Second Ave. and 10th St., is the oldest structure in the East Village and the second oldest church in the city. Built in 1799 (with the steeple added in 1828), it was badly damaged twice by fires in the late 1970s. Fully restored now, it continues a wide variety of cultural activities. There is a plaque on the church wall noting that four trees in honor of W.H. Auden, Paul Blackburn, Frank O'Hara, and Michael Scholnick have been planted in the yard.

This Episcopal church's liberal attitude toward artists began long ago. In the first half of the century, Isadora Duncan, Carl Sandburg, Kahlil Gibran, Harry Houdini, Frank Lloyd Wright, and William Carlos Williams spoke or performed here. W.H. Auden was a parishioner. (How Houdini escaped the church remains a secret.)

The St. Mark's Poetry Project began in the mid-1960s when Paul Blackburn helped set up poetry readings here after the closing of Café Le Metro. Joel Oppenheimer was the first director, Anne Waldman his assistant. So many poets of the New York School, Black Mountain, and Beat groups have read here in the past thirty years that a list of them would make up a Who's Who of contemporary poetry.

For decades a mimeograph machine was available for use by scores of little magazines and book publishers, and *The World* magazine is still published here. Each year on New Year's Day a mammoth poetry marathon is held to raise money for the Poetry Project. Readers from Ashbery to Zedd have performed. On Saturday, April 12, 1997 a memorial service for Allen Ginsberg was held before a packed house of mourners. Eulogies were provided by friends such as Amiri Baraka, Gregory Corso, Peter Orlovsky, Patti Smith, Lou Reed, Ron Padgett, and Larry Rivers.
Continue north on Second Ave. to the corner of 12th St.

14   Phoenix Theater

At 189 Second Ave. was the Phoenix Theater, now called Village East Cinemas. Built in 1926 as the Yiddish Art Theatre, it anchored the north end of what was then called the Jewish Rialto. Seating 1,100, it was one of the largest theaters for Yiddish-language actors. As Yiddish-language theaters declined, the theater reorganized as the Phoenix Theater in 1953, with avant-garde work and revivals: Samuel Beckett and Eugene Ionesco plays, Luigi Pirandello's *Six Characters in Search of an Author,* and George Bernard Shaw's *Saint Joan,* to name a few. They had a hit with Montgomery Clift in Chekhov's *The Sea Gull* in 1954. In the late 1960s and throughout the 1970s the tradition continued as the Entermedia Theater with off-Broadway openings of *Oh! Calcutta!* in 1969, *Grease* in 1972, and *The Best Little Whorehouse in Texas* in 1978. Now converted into a multi-screen theater, it retains its Neo-Moorish architecture. Look for the cornerstone with the date May 23, 1926 in English and Hebrew. People who go to films in the theater on the top floor can still see the beautiful stained glass ceiling from the original Yiddish Art Theatre

For three days in December 1978 the Nova Convention took place here, an avant-garde performance extravaganza in honor of William S. Burroughs, organized by poet John Giorno and emceed by Laurie Anderson. Performers: John Cage, Merce Cunningham, Patti Smith, Frank Zappa, and Burroughs himself, the real star of the show. Hundreds came to see the man who had coined the phrase "heavy metal" in *Naked Lunch,* invented the name "Steely Dan" (a dildo in the same book), and influenced David Bowie to use the cut-up method for the lyrics of *Diamond Dogs.*

Walk one more block north on Second Ave. and turn left across 13th St. to Third Ave. On the way you'll pass Emma Goldman's home at 208 E. 13th St. (See the plaque which has recently been put on the building where the anarchist advocate of free love and speech lived.) Turn right on Third Ave. to the Varieties Theater.

15   Varieties Theater

At 110-112 Third Ave. is the Varieties Theater, one of the last survivors of the early days of cinema. Built around the turn of the century, it predates the more opulent movie palaces of the 1920s. Its marquee has both neon and incandescent light bulbs and is a treasure of the neighborhood. Kerouac took Joyce Johnson here to see *The Sweet Smell of Success* just after his success with *On the Road.* "Don't be afraid—I won't go to the men's room and leave you," he reassured her. It used to be a place that derelicts went to

keep warm, and then for years it was a soft porn theater. Now it has been reborn as an off-Broadway venue with works by Woody Allen and Neil Simon. Film fans might recall the marquee as the same one below which Robert De Niro picks up Jody Foster in *Taxi Driver.*
Stop near the southwest corner of Third Ave. and 14th St.

16   Third Avenue Bars

This used to be the area of cheap Third Avenue bars. They had the working-class camaraderie in which Kerouac seemed to feel most at home "…men are all roaring in clink bonk glass brass-foot barrail 'where ya goin' excitement." The elevated train overhead made the area dim and sooty regardless of the time of day. The Met Supermarket between 14th and 15th St. at 137 Third Ave. was once the site of the Garden Bar where, said Kerouac, "you can do fantastic sprawling dances in the dim back room."

17   Con Ed Building

The Con Ed Building is at the corner of E. 14th St. and Irving Place. In "Manhattan Thirties Flash," Ginsberg describes the "Con Ed skyscraper clock-head gleaming gold-lit at sun dusk."
Walk one very long block to the west on 14th St. and turn left on Fourth Ave. which stretches for only six blocks south of this point; the rest of what was once Fourth Ave. was renamed Park Ave. South. Walk south two blocks on Fourth Ave. and stop at the corner of 12th St.

18   Book Row

The four blocks along Fourth Ave. between E. 9th St. and E. 13th St. was once known as "Book Row." In the 1940s and 1950s there were twenty-two used bookstores here. Kerouac wrote to Alfred Kazin in 1949 that he went to these bookstores to build a collection of classics with the advance he got from Harcourt for *The Town and the City.* "Instead I wound up being depressed at the sight of vast piles of useless and meaningless dusty literature . . . "

One by one the bookstores closed. The only one left is The Strand on Broadway at 12th St. Don't miss the rare book department on the second floor where many vintage Beat books are secreted. The entrance to the rare book department is a doorway to the left of the main entrance.
Walk south on Fourth Ave. to No. 108.

19 Alfred Leslie

In January 1959, Alfred Leslie's loft, where the film *Pull My Daisy* was shot, was at 108 4th Ave. The lofts, now gone, were above the frame shop at this address today. Leslie put slugs in the circuit board to avoid blowing the fuses with the enormous lights then needed for indoor filming. The film, based on act three of Kerouac's play, *The Beat Generation,* was produced by Robert Frank and Alfred Leslie for $15,000, paying five dollars a day to "actors" David Amram, Richard Bellamy, Gregory Corso, Ginsberg, Sally Gross, Peter Orlovsky, Larry Rivers, and Delphine Seyrig. The music was by David Amram. Kerouac spontaneously improvised the narration on the soundtrack while watching the film and listening to Amram's music on a headset. Although he reluctantly made a few takes of the narrative, the first one was the best, as he thought it would be.

Continue down 4th Ave. to 10th St. Turn left to the old row of buildings on the south side of the street.

20 Tenth Street Galleries/Tenth Street Coffee House

The Tenth Street Galleries were located on both sides of the short block of E. 10th St. between Third and Fourth Aves. For a period in the mid-1950s the most avant-garde art in America was shown in a dozen galleries here, on a street until then occupied only by pawnshops, pool rooms, and sheet metal shops. Cheap rents and larger work spaces attracted many Abstract Expressionist painters. The art critic Harold Rosenberg lived nearby at 117 E. 10th St. He and Clement Greenberg are credited (or blamed) with bringing the new art to the public's attention. Most of the galleries were cooperative ventures by artists to show their own work. Each usually had their own show every two years. Frank O'Hara was an important link between artists and poets in the East Village, and openings here were attended by many Beats, including Kerouac. Several of the galleries also had poetry and jazz. At that time, Alfred Barr, the director of the Museum of Modern Art, wrote: "The 10th Street galleries seem to be of great importance as an incubating center for young artists." (Quite an understatement, considering that he was witnessing the birth of Abstract Expressionism.)

The galleries on the south side of the street between Third to Fourth Aves. included:

Gallery Grimand at 96 E. 10th St. was founded in 1958. This building has been torn down and replaced by the large apartment building on the corner.

Camino Gallery at 92 E. 10th St. was a co-op founded in March

1956. (This building was also torn down.)

Tanager Gallery at 90 E. 10th St. was a co-op founded in 1952. Its members included Rudolph Burckhardt, Willem de Kooning, Philip Guston, Al Held, Alex Katz, Philip Pearlstein, and Tom Wesselmann. This building is still standing at the end of the row of townhouses. Imagine the whole block of buildings like this one with galleries in the basements as well as the parlor floors.

Willem de Kooning lived at 88 E. 10th St. in one of the buildings. He lived here before the influx of the Tenth Street Galleries, and he attracted them. Here in the early 1960s, Elaine de Kooning befriended Beat poet Ray Bremser, and literally bailed him out of trouble several times.

Stryke Gallery was at 86 E. 10th St. This building is still here.

Area Gallery was at 80 E. 10th St. (1958). This building has been torn down and replaced by the Atlas Barber School.

The storefront that now is the right half of the Atlas Barber School was the Tenth Street Coffee House owned by Mickey Ruskin from 1960 until 1962 (when he bought the larger Les Deux Megots). There were poetry readings organized by Chester Anderson, Howard Ant, and Ree Dragonette. Monday readings were open-mic nights. Wednesdays were for invited poets, including Carol Bergé, Marguerite Harris, Jackson MacLow, and Diane Wakoski.

All the galleries on the north side between Third and Fourth Aves. have been torn down. They included:

March Gallery at 95 E. 10th St., founded in 1957.

Brata Gallery at 89 E. 10th St., founded in December 1957. This is where David Amram and Kerouac gave their first poetry and jazz readings. Later the Aegis Gallery took over the space and the Brata moved to 56 Third Ave.

Walk back to Fourth Ave., turn left, and stop just around the corner.

21   Artist's Club/Reuben Gallery

A building that once housed the Artist's Club has been replaced by a check-cashing business at 73 Fourth Ave. near E. 10th St. On December 31, 1958 the cast party for Robert Frank's film, *Pull My Daisy,* was held here. The famous image of a disheveled Kerouac in a crowd with someone holding a doll was taken that night. The club was a gathering place for the Abstract Expressionists throughout the 1950s.

A little further south on Fourth Ave. is No. 61.

The Reuben Gallery was opened in a loft at 61 Fourth Ave. The gallery had Happenings by Red Grooms and Alan Kaprow.

Kaprow, who developed this art form and coined the term "Happening," staged "18 Happenings in Six Parts" here in the fall of 1959. They combined music, visual arts, drama, the spoken word, and audience participation. Kaprow once wrote that "a walk down 14th Street is more amazing than any masterpiece of art," and the Happening was his attempt to recreate such experience. Later, Happenings merged into street theater, and street theater in the revolutionary Sixties became real action in the streets. As part of the Sixties' counter-culture, Happenings inspired the Situationists in Europe as well as student uprisings in Paris '68 and the "Prague Spring." It should be noted, however, that Happenings were not the only use of audience participation for revolutionary purposes. The Living Theatre's *Paradise Now* led theater audiences singing and naked into the street. For this they were later busted in Avignon and other far places.

From here walk past the large black cube sculpture, The Alamo, on the pedestrian island to the corner of Lafayette St. and Astor Place.

22 Ted Joans

Ted Joans had a loft in this building at 12 Astor Place. He would meet Kerouac, buy a bottle at the liquor store here, and share it on their way to the Five Spot a few blocks away. This made it easier to nurse along an expensive drink at the club, listening to a night of jazz.

Return to Lafayette St. and walk south towards the Public Theatre banners. There's great New York history here, but very little having to do with the Beat Generation. Colonnade Row, directly across the street from the Public Theatre, was built in 1833 as the home of the wealthy Astors, Vanderbilts, and Delanos. John Jacob Astor built the Astor Library and gave it to the city as the first free library. It's now the Public Theatre.

23 Public Theatre

This building at 425 Lafayette St. was remodeled as a theater in 1967, housing Joseph Papp's Public Theatre. What is now the Anspacher Theater was the main reading room of the library. The most established of the avant-garde theaters in the area, it is home to the New York Shakespeare Festival. Broadway plays have opened here, including *A Chorus Line, Hair,* and *That Championship Season. No Place to Be Somebody* won the Pulitzer Prize after running here at a financial loss. The Public Theatre has had poetry readings by Anne Waldman and Ginsberg, and performances by Lou Reed and Laurie Anderson.

Continue down Lafayette St. for four blocks to the entrance of the Bleecker St. subway station.

24   Bleecker Street IRT Subway Station

The Bleecker Street IRT Subway Station at Bleecker and Lafayette St. on the uptown side is where twenty-five-year-old William Cannastra was killed in a gruesome accident on October 12, 1950. Kerouac used Cannastra as model for his character Finistra in *Visions of Cody*. His death was also a central event in John Clellon Holmes' novel *Go*, but Holmes moved the accident to the 23rd Street station. Holmes wrote in *Go* that as the No. 6 subway train pulled out of the station, a drunken Agatson (Cannastra) "tried to climb out one of the windows of the train. But he miscalculated the speed, and before he could pull back, the wall of the tunnel struck his head and shoulders, and he was sucked out of the window, jammed downward among the wheels, and dragged for fifty feet." He died shortly afterward at Columbus Hospital (now Cabrini Medical Center). Three friends who were with him at the time said he was trying to get out to go to the Bleecker Street Tavern. In "Howl" Ginsberg refers to Cannastra who "fell out of the subway window, jumped in the filthy Passaic, leaped on negroes, cried all over the street, danced on broken wineglasses barefoot smashed phonograph records of nostalgic European 1930s German jazz finished the whiskey and threw up groaning into the bloody toilet . . ."

Turn left on Bleecker St. and walk east to the Bowery. If you're on the left side of the street it's one block; if you're on the right side of the street, it's three blocks. Directly across the Bowery is CBGBs.

25   CBGB-OMFUG

The rock club, CBGB-OMFUG, which moved to 315 Bowery in the early 1970s, takes its name from its music at the time: Country, Blue Grass, Blues, and Other Music For Uplifting Gourmandizers. Here the Ramones, Richard Hell and Television, Debbie Harry and Blondie, Patti Smith, David Byrne and the Talking Heads, the Plasmatics, and the Butthole Surfers engaged audiences with the first sounds of American punk rock. Slam dancing was created at CBGBs when performers began tossing themselves from the stage into the audience.

The club has always had strong ties to the literary community. When the St. Mark's Church suffered a disastrous fire, Helena Hughes organized a giant benefit here. Recently the club has offered readings by writers Herbert Huncke, Gregory Corso, and Allen Gins-

berg in the annex just to the right of the main band room.
Turn right and walk down the Bowery to Houston St.

26   Fred Bunz

The vacant lot on the southeast corner of Houston and Bowery
was a skid row hash house in the 1940s and 1950s run by a man
named Fred Bunz. Kerouac described Fred Bunz' diner as "the
great bum's Howard Johnsons of the Bowery." The menu was written on the window with soap. Pig brains were 15¢ and goulash a
quarter.
Continue down the Bowery for two blocks and stop at the large
building, No. 222.

27   William Burroughs

William Burroughs in "The Bunker."
Photo by Louis R. Cartwright.

William Burroughs lived at 222 Bowery from 1975 until 1981 in
an apartment nicknamed "The Bunker," so called because it had
no windows: It had been a YMCA locker room. The windowless
atmosphere was perfectly suited to Burroughs, the man so reclu-
sive he was called "El Hombre Invisible." Subterranean visitors included Ginsberg, Mick Jagger, and Andy Warhol. Victor Bockris
has detailed these years in his book, *With William Burroughs: A*
Report from the Bunker.
Retrace your steps back up the Bowery to Houston St. Walk
east on Houston one block and turn left at the next corner,
which is the intersection with Second Ave. Walk two blocks
north on Second Ave. to the corner of 2nd St. Stop at the corner
just before turning to the right.

28   Anthology Film Archives

At 32-34 Second Ave. on the southeast corner at 2nd St. is the Anthology Film Archives. Once an office for the courts, this building was beautifully renovated in 1979 and is devoted solely to avant-

Jonas Mekas and Edie Sedgwick introduce the first public appearance of Velvet Underground at Psychiatrist's Convention, New York, January 14, 1966.
Courtesy of the Anthology Film Archives, New York.

garde film. It contains archival storage for over ten thousand films, a library, and several theaters showing current and retrospective films. Founded by the independent filmmaker, Jonas Mekas, the archive was an outgrowth of his Filmmaker's Cinematheque and the Filmmaker's Cooperative. Here are stored and shown films by Kenneth Anger, Stan Brakhage, Jean Cocteau, Robert Frank, Man Ray, Harry Smith, Andy Warhol, and a legion of others. *Walk east on 2nd St. towards First Ave. to the gates of the cemetery on the left side of the street.*

29   New York City Marble Cemetery

The New York City Marble Cemetery at 52-74 E. 2nd St. is a private cemetery founded in 1832, containing the remains of many prominent New Yorkers. A favorite is the grave of one named Preserved Fish. In describing the view from the window of the apartment of San Remo habitué Bill Keck, Allen Ginsberg wrote about this cemetery in *Journals Early Fifties Early Sixties.* "His loft has a window on the stairway overlooking a cemetery—stairway dark & old & deserted, rubbish filled—3 flights in unused bldg. $15 a month rent pipes electric up from next floor, has candles also & kerosene lamp. Tacked on wall—Song by Moondog."
Continue east on 2nd St. and turn left onto First Ave. Stop in front of No. 41.

30   Bill Keck/Norman Mailer

Bill Keck was described by Kerouac as the quintessential Subterranean, called Fritz Nicholas in the novel *The Subterraneans.* He is called Dick Beck in *Book of Dreams.* Both Kerouac and Allen Ginsberg stayed at Keck's apartment in the back of this building overlooking the old cemetery. In "Howl" Ginsberg saw the "backyard green tree cemetery dawns . . ." Keck gave Ginsberg his first peyote and made friends with Julian Beck, Judith Malina, Philip Lamantia, and Carl Solomon. He was active in avant-garde theater, having played Galba the Gladiator in an anarchist production of *Faustina*. He also took part in the very first productions of the Living Theatre staged in the home of Beck and Malina.

Bill Keck, ca. 1953.
©Allen Ginsberg Trust. Courtesy of Fahey/Klein Gallery, Los Angeles.

In 1951-1952, Norman Mailer lived on the top floor of this tall, red brick tenement building at 41 First Ave. He renovated the apartment, doing his own plumbing and electrical work. He gave some giant parties here for people like Marlon Brando, Montgomery Clift, Lillian Hellman, James Jones, and Vance Bourjaily. And here Mailer wrote most of *The Deer Park*.

Dan Wolf lived in the identical building next door to Mailer at 39 First Ave. In 1955 Wolf, Mailer, and Edwin Fancher founded the *Village Voice*. Wolf and Mailer visited each other by walking across the roof. When Mailer moved to No. 41 he was beginning to date Adele Morales, a Peruvian painter who was ending a relationship with Kerouac. She had previously dated Ed Fancher, soon to be Mailer's *Village Voice* partner. Within a few months she rented the apartment next door to Wolf, and shortly after that moved in with Mailer. She became his second and most famous wife when he

stabbed her on November 22, 1960. Morales dropped charges against him and he was sent to Bellevue for a psychiatric examination, then released on probation. (He's still at large.)
Continue north on First Ave. to 3rd St., turn left toward Second Ave., and stop at No. 48.

31 Artist's Studio

In the late 1950s, the brick townhouse at 48 E. 3rd St. was the Artist's Studio, an informal poetry and jazz center run by black artist and writer, George Nelson Preston. In the front room behind the picture window was a large open space that served as auditorium for poetry readings in 1959. Kerouac read from *On the Road* here, and was photographed standing with outstretched arms. That photograph has been much reproduced and was used as the cover for *The Beat Scene*, an early anthology published by Corinth Books in 1960. Ferlinghetti did a painting of Kerouac based on this photo, and it's on the cover of the City Lights edition of Kerouac's *Pomes All Sizes.* Ray Bremser, Gregory Corso, Diane di Prima, Allen Ginsberg, Ted Joans, LeRoi Jones, Frank O'Hara, and Peter Orlovsky read at the Artist's Studio.
Turn right on Second Ave. for a block and stop at No. 81.

32 Dodie Muller

One of Kerouac's girlfriends, Dodie Muller, lived in a loft at 81 Second Ave. in the late 1950s. She had the second floor above the storefront and rented from a rabbi who lived above her. In an interview Kerouac said his mother didn't like Dodie because "she has long, long hair and doesn't tie it up. Because she likes to go barefoot. Because she's an Indian. She's 95 per cent Indian, and my mother calls her *la sauvage*—'the savage.' She's a very Bohemian painter, you know. She's teaching me how to paint." Kerouac continued drawing and painting all his life. The first show of his art was organized by Ed Adler at New York University during the 1994 conference on the Beat Generation. Kerouac met Irish writer Brendan Behan while visiting Muller here.
Return to E. 4th St. and then turn west. Stop at the first theater on the right side of the street, The Red Room, 85 E. 4th St.

33 Off-Off-Broadway Theater Row

Experimental theater groups were very active in the East Village even before the 1950s. They used the theaters of the Yiddish playhouses nearby, and many are still clustered along a small stretch of E. 4th St. between the Bowery and 2nd Ave. Some of these were:

The Downtown Theater at 85 E. 4th St. In the 1950s it produced

such plays as George Bernard
Shaw's *Arms and the Man* and
Sartre's *The Flies*. In the 1960s it
was renamed The East End
Theater. Diane di Prima and
Alan Marlowe's New York Poets
Theater began producing plays
here in 1962. Plays by Robert
Duncan, LeRoi Jones, Michael
McClure, and Frank O'Hara
were all performed here. The
theater is now named The The-
atre Red Room, at E. 4th St. near
2nd Ave.

62 E. 4th St.
Photo by Bill Morgan.

The Fourth Street Theatre at
83 E. 4th St. The 1955-1956 sea-
son included Anton Chekhov's
The Cherry Orchard, The Seagull, and *Uncle Vanya* with Franchot
Tone. Other productions starred Eva Gabor and Patrick O'Neal.
Later in 1966 the theater was called Atelier East, and for a short
time there were poetry readings carried over from the Café Le
Metro and Les Deux Megots, before the St. Mark's Poetry Project
was established. Carol Bergé, Paul Blackburn, Ted Enslin, Jerome
Rothenberg, and Gilbert Sorrentino read here. It is now the T.
Schreiber Studio.

The New York Theater Workshop at 79 E. 4th St. has also been
called The Truck and Warehouse.

La Mama Experimental Theatre Club at 74A E. 4th St. In 1962,
Ellen Stewart, inspired by the Café Cino in Greenwich Village,
opened her theater in the basement of a building at 321 E. 9th St.
After several moves she settled in this location in 1969. Off-off-
Broadway writers such as Diane di Prima, Jean-Claude van Itallie,
Paul Foster, Ruth Yorck, Tom Eyen, Julie Bovasso, Jack Micheline,
Harold Pinter, Sam Shepard, and Lanford Wilson (*Balm in Gilead*)
have had work staged by La Mama. And Harvey Fierstein's *Torch
Song Trilogy* premiered as three separate one-act plays.

The Royal Playhouse was at 62 E. 4th St. in 1958. In the mid-
sixties it was re-named Theatre 62 and is now the Duo. It is distinguished by the unusual use of an exterior circular fire escape in
the front.

*Continue west on E. 4th St. to the next corner where the Bowery
becomes E. 3rd and then 4th Ave. Turn right and stop by the
large apartment building between E. 4th St. and E. 5th St.*

34   Five Spot

The Five Spot, the bebop and jazz mecca at 5 Cooper Square, was once located on the Bowery between E. 4th St. and E. 5th St. The whole block was torn down and replaced by a fourteen-story high-rise apartment building. Two brothers, Iggie and Joe Termini, opened the bar in the mid-1940s and it was just another Bowery flophouse. And so it remained for several years, until artists, poets, and musicians started coming in the 1950s due to the Terminis' generosity. From the start they had a great, free jukebox. And every-one came to drink 20-cent beers and listen to David Amram, Don Cherry, Ornette Coleman, John Coltrane, Billie Holiday, Charlie Mingus, Thelonious Monk, Sonny Rollins, and Cecil Taylor. Kerouac wrote in *Lonesome Traveler,* "If you know the proprietor you sit down at the table free with a beer, but if you don't know him you can sneak in and stand by the ventilator and listen."

One wall was plastered with posters for art shows, poetry read-ings, and jam sessions. Regulars included artists Willem de Kooning, Grace Hartigan, Alfred Leslie, Larry Rivers, David Smith, and Harry Smith. Rivers came to play jazz saxophone. Writers at the bar included Allen Ginsberg, LeRoi Jones, Kerouac, Kenneth Koch (who read poetry accompanied by Larry Rivers' music), Frank O'Hara, and Dan Propper (who read with Thelonious Monk in 1958).

According to Kerouac, Ginsberg loved Lester Young's music so much that he fell to his knees while talking to him in the back room. LeRoi Jones said that "when Thelonious Monk came in for his historic eighteen-week stay with John Coltrane, I was there al-most every night." Frank O'Hara wrote a poem about the death of Billie Holiday which ends: " . . . and thinking of / leaning on the john door in the 5 SPOT / while she whispered a song along the keyboard / to Mal Waldron and everyone and I stopped breath-ing." (Mal Waldron was Billie Holiday's pianist.) In 1962 the Five Spot moved to newer quarters at 2 St. Mark's Place and stayed there for several years until finally closing.
Continue north and stop at No. 27 in the next block between E. 5th St. and E. 6th St.

35   LeRoi and Hettie Cohen Jones

LeRoi and Hettie Cohen Jones moved to the top floor of 27 Cooper Square at 5th St. in early 1962. It was a skylighted garret across the street from a Harz Mountain Bird Food factory (now replaced by the *Village Voice* offices). The Joneses continued the publishing they had begun on Morton St. on E.14th St. While living here LeRoi wrote one of his most important books, *Blues People.* LeRoi

left Hettie and his children here in 1965, moved back to Harlem, and later to his hometown of Newark where he became a radical African American and renamed himself Amiri Baraka. Hettie Jones described their lives here in her wonderful memoir *How I Became Hettie Jones*.
Just a few doors to the north is No. 35

36 Diane di Prima

Between 1962 and 1964 Diane di Prima lived at 35 Cooper Square, where she edited and published an important mimeograph newsletter with LeRoi Jones, *The Floating Bear*. During this same period di Prima had a child by Jones, her neighbor at the time. Many of the books for her Poet's Press were edited in this apartment as well. She published Kirby Doyle, Herbert Huncke, Clive Matson, A.B. Spellman, and Philip Whalen, as well as herself.
Turn right onto E. 6th St. and immediately turn left at Tara Shevchenko Place. (Not one New Yorker in a million would know the name of this street.) You're now facing the last stop on this tour, perhaps much to everyone's relief.

37 McSorley's Old Ale House

McSorley's Old Ale House at 15 E. 7th St. is the oldest bar in the city, founded in 1854. It certainly hasn't changed since Kerouac's days, except in one way — until 1971, no women were allowed. Four U.S. Presidents, including Lincoln and Kennedy, visited this bar; John Sloan painted it and Brendan Behan considered it one of his favorites. And e.e. cummings wrote a poem about it beginning: "i was sitting in mcsorley's. outside it was New York and beauti- / fully snowing. / Inside snug and evil . . ."

In more recent times it was a hang-out for poet Paul Blackburn. Once in 1962, LeRoi Jones, writer Gil Sorrentino, and artist Basil King were beaten up by ten men outside the bar. The neighborhood is much safer now and the bar is full of NYU students in the evenings. Have a glass of McSorley's ale, and drink in the drunken air and old times.

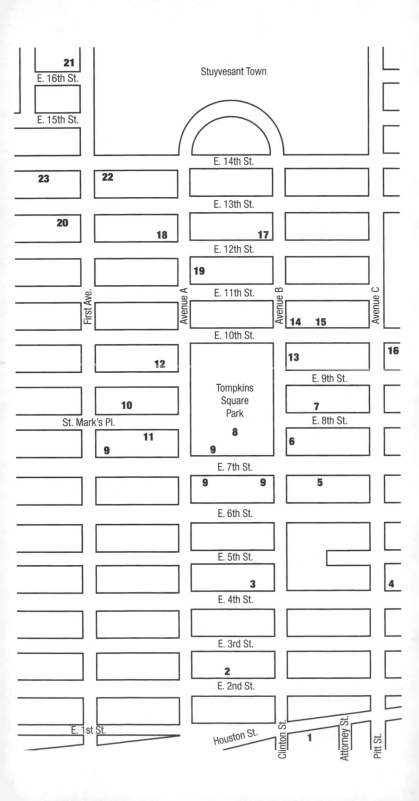

Allen Ginsberg and Peter Orlovsky on E. 10th St., 1966.
Courtesy of United Press International.

East Village
Tour 2

Length of tour: 2 hours
Subway: F train to 2nd Ave.
Bus: M9, M14 (Avenue A or B routes), M21
Begin this tour on the north side of E. Houston, near the corner of Avenue B. Look across Houston at the building with the bright yellow grocery and tire repair signs.

1   Diane di Prima
Diane di Prima lived in the large, six-floor brick building at 309 E. Houston St. in 1961. Here she published the first fifteen issues of

The Floating Bear, one of the seminal far-out underground poetry magazines of the decade. *The Floating Bear* was named after a boat Winnie-the-Pooh made out of a honey pot in A.A. Milne's classic children's book. Di Prima and LeRoi Jones were the editors and publishers of what soon became a newsletter for experimental poets. Besides the editors, contributors were William Burroughs, Gregory Corso, Robert Creeley, Ed Dorn, Allen Ginsberg, Michael McClure, Frank O'Hara, Charles Olson, Lew Welch, Philip Whalen, and numberless others.

On October 18, 1961 several FBI agents came here to arrest Diane di Prima on the charge of sending obscene material (*The Floating Bear*) through the mail. She eluded the agents at the house, but turned herself in later that day. The grand jury failed to find grounds to indict the publishers, but defending themselves put di Prima and Jones in debt. (As in all such cases, the debts incurred by the defendants were part of the FBI strategy to persecute dissidents.) The alleged obscene issue contained William Burroughs' "Routine" and LeRoi Jones' "The System of Dante's Hell."
Walk north on Avenue B one block to E. 2nd St. and turn left for a half-block to No. 170.

2   Allen Ginsberg and Peter Orlovsky

Peter Orlovsky (in back), Carol Heller (Peter's girlfriend), Lafcadio Orlovsky, and Elise Cowen.
©Allen Ginsberg Trust. Courtesy of Fahey/Klein Gallery, Los Angeles.

Allen Ginsberg and Peter Orlovsky lived in apartment 16 of the large brick and stone building at 170 E. 2nd St. from August 1958 until March 23, 1961, when they left for India via Tangier. For $60 per month they shared four rooms in "The Croton" as it is called. After Spartan conditions in Paris, they were delighted with the amenities: steam heat, hot water, refrigerator, and new stove. The building overlooked an all-night Jewish bakery and was only a few blocks from Orchard St. where Ginsberg's mother had lived as a girl just arrived from Russia.

Here, as everywhere that Ginsberg lived, he was surrounded by countless friends. He found Herbert Huncke an apartment here and Bob Kaufman also moved in. Ginsberg saw much of Alex Trocchi, Irving Rosenthal, Kerouac, Lucien Carr, Ray Bremser, and Timothy Leary here. Ginsberg had sought out Leary (at the time a psychology professor at Harvard) in Cambridge and invited him to come to New York to experiment with psilocybin. While at this apartment Leary and Ginsberg "started planning the psychedelic revolution," said Leary. Once under the influence of psilocybin, Kerouac took Leary out into the street for a game of football with a loaf of bread. Ginsberg remembers this was the day Kerouac said the immortal words, "Walking on water wasn't built in a day." Elise Cowen, a bright girl in love with Ginsberg, also found an apartment in the building above him.

In this apartment Ginsberg wrote his great poem, "Kaddish," a prayer for his dead mother, Naomi. "TV Baby Poem" and the latter poem "I Beg You Come Back and Be Cheerful" are grounded in this apartment, beginning, "Tonite I got hi in the window of my apartment / chair at 3 A.M. / gazing at Blue incandescent torches / bright-lit street below . . ."

Marie Orlovsky, Peter's younger sister studying to be a pediatric nurse, was sleeping over one night when a drunken Kerouac burst into her room and scared her. When Ginsberg scolded him for his antics he laughingly rolled on the floor and uttered more immortal words: "Ginsberg, you're a hairy loss!" This was also the first stop that Kerouac, Lew Welch, and Albert Saijo made when they drove across the country from California in Welch's Jeep. They presented Ginsberg with a wood cross stolen from a roadside memorial on Route 66; it became a fixture on Ginsberg's wall. *Continue across 2nd St. to Avenue A, turn right two blocks, turn right again, and walk east on 4th St. to No. 229.*

3   Diane di Prima

Diane di Prima lived in the tall, narrow brick building at 229 E. 4th St. in 1961 and 1962. Here she published issues 16-24 of *The Floating Bear* with an all-star cast of helpers. Sometimes the young jazz pianist, Cecil Taylor, would stop by to run the mimeo. This was about the time he was recording *The New Breed*. Fred Herko, a dancer who committed suicide by dancing out an open window, collated the issues, and dancer James Waring typed.

Continue 1 1/2 blocks east on 4th St. and turn left on Avenue C for one block. Turn right onto 5th St. and stop at the vacant lot on your right just past the corner.

4 Allen Ginsberg and Peter Orlovsky

Jack Kerouac visiting Allen Ginsberg at 704 E. 5th St., 1964.
©Allen Ginsberg Trust. Courtesy of Fahey/Klein Gallery, Los Angeles.

From January 1964 until the summer of 1965, Allen Ginsberg and Peter Orlovsky lived on the top floor in apartment 5A of a six-story building that once stood here at 704 E. 5th St. Ginsberg had a three-room apartment here for $35 per month, overlooking the Wall Street skyline to the south. The neighborhood was dingy and crime-ridden, but the apartment was bright and decorated with Chinese scrolls and Indian prints (Ginsberg and Orlovsky had just returned from two years in India and the Far East). Gregory Corso lived here for a while, "right in the heart of the horror," as he described it. Painter Robert LaVigne and Peter's brother, Julius

Orlovsky, also stayed here at length.

Here Ginsberg wrote "Waking in New York": "And here am on the sixth floor cold / March 5th Street old building plaster / apartments in ruin, super he drunk . . ." and also "Morning" in which he describes the noise of "garbage can lids music over / truck whine on E. 5th St."

The last photographs Ginsberg took of Kerouac were in this apartment in the fall of 1964, showing a bloated Kerouac, a "corpulent red-faced W.C. Fields" in Ginsberg's words. Here also Ginsberg wrote a screenplay version of "Kaddish" with Robert Frank. Then he worked on a campaign to protest obscenity charges against Lenny Bruce. Most of Ginsberg's friends found their way to this apartment at one time or another, including Ken Kesey, Andy Warhol, and Timothy Leary. While he was in Eastern Europe in the summer of 1965, the city condemned the property and turned off the heat and hot water. They gave Orlovsky $100 to relocate.

Return to Avenue C and continue north for two blocks to 7th St. Turn left to No. 206.

5   Allen Ginsberg

Ginsberg lived in apartment 16 on the third floor in the back of this yellow brick building at 206 E. 7th St. from October 1952 until late 1953, paying $33.80 per month. Ginsberg's most famous photographs of Beat writers were taken here. The cover photograph of Kerouac on the fire escape and one of Burroughs sitting behind a row of books were taken here in the fall of 1953.

William Burroughs, 1953.
©Allen Ginsberg Trust. Courtesy of Fahey/Klein Gallery, Los Angeles.

Burroughs had returned from Mexico and South America after he killed his wife, Joan. He hoped for a romantic liaison with Ginsberg. Although Ginsberg felt close to Burroughs, he wasn't interested sexually. Here, the two put together the manuscripts of *Queer* and *The Yage Letters*, and Burroughs conceived the rough ideas for the first routines in *Naked Lunch*. The laundry lines in the back courtyard of the building inspired some passages for *Interzone*. Burroughs left in 1953 and headed out for a long stay lost in the interzones of Tangier and Europe.

William Burroughs on the roof of 206 E. 7th St., 1953.
©Allen Ginsberg Trust. Courtesy of Fahey/Klein Gallery, Los Angeles.

Ginsberg was working as a copyboy at the *New York World-Telegram* at this time and later took a job with George Fine Market Research doing consumer surveys about cosmetics and deodorants. Gregory Corso lived here with Ginsberg for a while, and other irregular visitors were Alan Ansen, Lucien Carr, and John Clellon Holmes. Holmes and Kerouac had a reconciliation at this apartment, which Kerouac described in *The Subterraneans*.

Allen Ginsberg overlooking St. Brigid's, 1953.
©Allen Ginsberg Trust. Courtesy of Fahey/Klein Gallery, Los Angeles.

Kerouac had a relationship with Alene Lee, who lived a few blocks away on Avenue A, and their story is retold in *The Subterraneans*. Several scenes are set in Ginsberg's apartment here. One of the episodes is based on a true story: Gregory Corso, Alene Lee, and Kerouac stole an Italian peddler's pushcart from Washington Square, and Corso pushed Kerouac and Lee in it across town to Ginsberg's apartment. In the morning when Ginsberg saw the stolen pushcart in front of his apartment he was livid, thinking of the poor owner of the cart as well as how his landlord might react. Kerouac threw down his key to Ginsberg's apartment and left, but within a few days the matter was forgotten and Kerouac had his key again.

William Burroughs and Alene Lee, 1953
©Allen Ginsberg Trust. Courtesy of Fahey/Klein Gallery, Los Angeles.

In "My Alba," a dejected Ginsberg wrote: "Now that I've wasted / five years in Manhattan / life decaying / talent a blank . . . " He was soon to leave this apartment for California and Mexico and wouldn't return to New York until he had written "Howl."
Continue west on 7th St. to the next corner and turn right onto Avenue B.

6   St. Brigid's Church

On the corner of Avenue B and E. 8th St. stands St. Brigid's Church, a landmark often referred to in the writings of poets. Frank O'Hara lived across the park on E. 9th St., and with Bill Berkson wrote *Hymns of St. Bridget*, published in 1974. Many of the poems mention the slender steeples that once graced the belfries, removed in the 1970s. *Lunch Poems,* published by City Lights Books in 1965, contains a poem called "Steps" in which he writes, "How funny you are today New York / like Ginger Rogers in *Swingtime* / and St. Bridget's [sic] steeple leaning a little to the left . . . " It was probably because the steeple did lean a little that it was removed. (O'Hara incorrectly calls the church St. Bridget's. The legend of St. Brigid is the story of an Irish girl who disfigures herself to discourage the men attracted to her.) Kerouac also wrote about walking past the church on his trips between Alene Lee's and Ginsberg's apartments in *The Subterraneans.*
Look down 8th St. just to the left of the church. David Amram's former apartment was half-way down on the left, just past the old, yellow brick synagogue. There isn't anything left of it but a vacant lot.

7   David Amram

When David Amram, a jazz French horn player, returned from Europe in 1955, he found an apartment at 319 E. 8th St. While living here he went to the Manhattan School of Music on the G.I. Bill and studied with Gunther Schuller. He also began performing with jazz greats like Charles Mingus, Thelonious Monk, and Dizzy Gillespie. He worked the graveyard shift at the post office and spent his free time immersed in music. During these early years he began long friendships with many writers, among them Philip Lamantia, Kerouac, and Howard Hart.

8   Tompkins Square

The East Village counterpart of Greenwich Village's Washington Square is Tompkins Square. This beautiful 16-acre park figures in Kerouac's novel *The Subterraneans.* "As we're walking along the benches of the church park sad park of the whole summer season" begins Kerouac's description of going through this park with Alene Lee (Mardou Fox in the book). They were going between her Paradise Alley apartment and Ginsberg's apartment on E. 7th St. during the late summer of 1953. (The church is St. Brigid's.)

During the 1960s the park became the hub of radical cultural and political events. This was the center of the action, from Hare Krishna gatherings to marijuana Smoke-Ins. The Grateful Dead, The Fugs, and Country Joe and the Fish performed in the bandshell, built in 1965, near the E. 7th St. side. Earlier, Franz Kline, Mark Rothko, and other New York Abstract Expressionists lived near the square.

In 1966 Ginsberg wrote about the park in a travel guide for librarians. He called Tompkins Square "A raw place in New York, one where the cement skin of the city is bruised. . . . Conditions of megalopolitan grandeur and decay are best observed in this area, and hints of a new consciousness emergent in American culture can be sniffed out on the adjacent streets. The librarian must be sure, if he is attempting to score for marijuana, that he has proper identification as an intellectual and a librarian, so that he be received with calm and amity."

The park has had a hot history. In 1874 it was the site of the first organized labor demonstration in the city. Labor leader Samuel Gompers was injured when the carpenters union clashed with police. In the 1960s trouble started when the older neighborhood Ukrainian community complained about the noise created by Hippies in the park. The Hippies took over the park, but Puerto Rican youths jumped in to fight them. The police were called out in force when vandals burning rubbish began setting fire to park benches. The most recent clash occurred in the late 1980s when the city tore down the bandshell and makeshift shacks built by squatters. The police overreacted to protests and the neighborhood polarized in two factions: some wanted the park to be open to all the people and some believed squatters had the right to take over public property for their private use. The park was closed for two years and completely renovated, with new playgrounds, benches, and a dog run. A curfew was also imposed and the park has once again become the center of the East Village community. *Return to the corner of 7th St. and Avenue B.*

9   Jack Kerouac

With the following portfolio of photographs in hand, we'll retrace a walk that Kerouac and Ginsberg made in the fall of 1953 across 7th St. from Ginsberg's apartment at No. 206 west to First Ave. Ginsberg snapped pictures of Kerouac as they walked. We've reassembled them in the order they were taken to provide a mini-photographic tour. The first photo, the cover of this

Avenue B and E. 7th St.
©Allen Ginsberg Trust. Courtesy of Fahey/ Klein Gallery, Los Angeles.

book, was taken on the fire escape at the rear of Ginsberg's apartment. When they reached his corner, Ginsberg snapped Kerouac as he passed in front of Vazac's bar. You can see the same stained glass windows in the bar today.

Continue further along 7th St. and stop just before the corner of Avenue A. Across the street you'll see the statue of Samuel Cox that shows above the head of Kerouac in the following picture.

Samuel Cox salutes Kerouac.
©Allen Ginsberg Trust. Courtesy of Fahey/Klein Gallery, Los Angeles.

Kerouac then paused to look into a window of a storefront that was once near this same corner. The photo looks eastward, back along the way we came.

Cross Avenue A, continue along 7th St. towards First Ave., and stop on the south side of the street across from St. Stanislaus Catholic Church. You can clearly see the church and rectory in the background. A statue of Pope John Paul II now stands just where Jack's head appears in the photograph.

Left: Window-shopping.
Right: At St. Stanislaus Catholic Church.
©Allen Ginsberg Trust. Courtesy of Fahey/Klein Gallery, Los Angeles.
Continue west along 7th St. and turn right onto First Ave. Walk one block north to St. Mark's Place, turn right again, and stop at No. 101.

10 Ted Berrigan

Ted Berrigan, who once ironically called himself "the last of the Beats," was a much-loved figure in the East Village poetry world. He and his wife, poet Alice Notley, lived in an apartment above the café and bookstore at 101 St. Mark's Place from the mid-1970s until his sudden death on July 4, 1983 at the age of 48. Like Kerouac, Berrigan's earliest influence came from reading Thomas Wolfe's novels. Later, he was drawn to the poetry of Frank O'Hara, John Ashbery, Kenneth Koch, and Paul Blackburn.

Ted Berrigan did one of the few in-depth interviews with Kerouac that focused on his writing rather than on his lifestyle. It was published in *The Paris Review* in 1968. Berrigan, along with Aram Saroyan and Duncan McNaughton, made the trip to Lowell after Kerouac had okayed their request for an interview. When they arrived, Kerouac's wife Stella almost kept them from coming in, thinking that they were three more wannabeats inspired by *On the Road* wanting to take Kerouac out on a binge. After the interview, Ted explained Kerouac's effect on young writers: "Jack gave you the sense that you could just be who you were and make a change in your life."

Berrigan, author of *The Sonnets*, *So Going Around Cities*, and *Selected Poems*, set many of his poems in this neighborhood. In a mock testimonial entitled "Last Poem" he notes the importance of this home base: "verbalized myself a place in society, 101 St. Marks Place, Apartment 12A, NYC, 10009."

When first in New York in the early 1960s, Berrigan edited *C* magazine for a younger generation of poets. While living here, he kept in contact with friends from his hometown of Tulsa: Ron Padgett, Dick Gallup, and Joe Brainard. Berrigan and Notley's small apartment served as a salon, their walls covered with artwork by friends Philip Guston, Larry Rivers, Joe Brainard, and George Schneeman. Their bookshelves overflowed with works by fellow poets. The door was open to younger writers, who received formal and informal training from Berrigan. His influence was far reaching, attested by tributes in *Nice to See You: Homage to Ted Berrigan*, edited by Anne Waldman.

Across the street from Berrigan's apartment at No. 108 is an old garage-type building.

11   Galerie Fantastique

In March 1956, Ted Joans opened the Galerie Fantastique, a quirky art gallery, at 108 St. Mark's Place. Joans was famous for his parties, such as the Beatnik birthday celebration held on July 25, 1959. Artists and writers as diverse as Robert Smithson, Robert Frank, Larry Poons, LeRoi Jones, Ginsberg, and Kerouac came to his combination apartment/gallery in this old storefront. Ted Joans made his name in the media as one of the original "Rent-a-Beatnik" poets. They rented themselves out as beatniks to wealthy uptown and suburban clients for their parties.

Turn left onto Avenue A and left once again at the next corner onto 9th St. Stop at No. 441.

12   Frank O'Hara

Frank O'Hara lived with Joe LeSueur on the second floor of this six-story brick tenement at 441 E. 9th St., from March 1959 through 1964. It was the typical Lower East Side apartment, complete with bathtub in the kitchen. The only distinction was that on O'Hara's walls were future museum pieces by Rivers, Hartigan, Mitchell, and de Kooning. This apartment proved to be a great inspiration for O'Hara. He wrote about the neighborhood, the park, stores, and churches that he could see from his window. In Diane di Prima's poem, "For Frank O'Hara, An Elegy" she wrote: " . . . I'd bring onion bread to 9th St. for Sunday brunch/our walks in Tompkins Square, St. Brigit's [sic] looming aside." In 1966 O'Hara was killed in a freak accident on Fire Island — he was run over by a dune-buggy taxi in the middle of the night on a deserted beach.

An air of mystery has come to enshroud what actually happened. *Enter the park at 9th St. and cross Tompkins Square from Avenue A to Avenue B. At Avenue B you'll find No. 145 directly in front of you to the left.*

13   Christodora House/Charlie Parker

Now a stylish apartment building, the Christodora House, 145 Avenue B at E. 9th St., was originally built in 1928 as a settlement house for the poor. In the third-floor concert hall a young neighborhood boy, George Gershwin, gave his first public recital. The first rally to legalize marijuana was held here in December 1964 by a group called LeMar (Legalize Marijuana). Ginsberg remembers that he and Ed Sanders were among a dozen demonstrators to picket in front of the welfare office in this building, the only federal offices they could find in the neighborhood. Over the years, the number of demonstrators grew and grew.

A few doors north on Avenue B is No. 151, between E. 9th and E. 10th Streets.

A plaque on this building commemorates Charlie "Bird" Parker's ground-floor residence at 151 Avenue B during 1950-1954. Each year the neighborhood holds a Charlie Parker festival in Tompkins Square, and the section of Avenue B in front of the building has been renamed Charlie Parker Way. Ginsberg visited Parker and met Thelonious Monk and other jazzists. When Ginsberg asked Monk what he thought of "Howl," he said, "It makes sense." (What kind of sense it made to him, we'll never know.)

Walk to the corner of Avenue B and 10th St. The building which contained No. 163 has been renovated, and the storefront with this number was removed. No. 163 would have been the left part of the ground floor facing Avenue B.

14   The Annex

During the 1960s, the Annex was located at 163 Avenue B. It was a bar appealing to a beer and peanuts crowd, as well as to neighborhood artists and poets. Someone once said the people who couldn't afford the Cedar Tavern came here. Guidebooks from the 1960s considered this a pretty dangerous place, but it was more likely that they were disconcerted by the presence of interracial couples around the bar. One such book states, "Negroes abound in the Annex, and like the white men around them they go there looking more for women than for drink." The bar was owned by Mickey Ruskin, later owner of Les Deux Megots Coffeehouse and Max's Kansas City.

Over the bar of the Annex was a sign: "ATTENTION WRITERS: All great American novels, distinguished short stories, and immortal poetry written in this bar must be completed, typed, and submitted before closing time."

After you have obeyed this sign, walk east on 10th St. towards Avenue C. Stop on the left in front of the lot where No. 383 would be. It is past the middle of the block and contains a casita, a Caribbean summer social club.

15 Peace Eye Book Store

Ed Sanders opened the Peace Eye Book Store here at 383 E. 10th St. in 1964. He said, "I deliberately picked the most remote, while at the same time groovy, location I could find — an old kosher butcher shop with mounds of chicken drippings on the floor." He left the "Strictly Kosher" sign in the window and added two hieroglyphic eyes of the ancient Egyptian sun-god Ra. The grand opening party attracted over 100 people. Sanders' idea was that everything could be sold as "literary curiosities." For example, a framed collection of pubic hair from sixteen leading poets, Ginsberg's cold cream jars, and even Ginsberg's beard (priced at $24.75) were available. Sanders published a "rare book catalog" listing all the esoteric items and written in the exquisite jargon of antiquarian book dealers. The catalog itself is now a collector's item. On opening day, the neighborhood kids threw firecrackers at people going in and out of the store until Ginsberg went outside, knelt in the street, and chanted in the midst of the mayhem, winning the kids over.

The store became an underground Mecca for poets, musicians, and activists. It was the home of the NYC LeMar group that had organized to legalize the use of marijuana. Here Ed Sanders, Tuli Kupferberg, Steve Weber, and Ken Weaver formed The Fugs, named after the euphemism Norman Mailer used in his book *The Naked and the Dead*. Sanders himself had no such reservations when he named his own literary magazine, *Fuck You: A Magazine of the Arts*. The police raided the bookshop on January 2, 1966, under the pretext of responding to a burglary. They charged Sanders with possession of obscene literature and lewd prints. Although the case was successfully defended by the ACLU, the confiscated evidence was never returned to Sanders, and this, in effect, put him out of business.

Continue on 10th St. across Avenue C to No. 408, a red brick apartment building on the right side of the street.

16   Allen Ginsberg and Peter Orlovsky

In 1965, while Ginsberg was on a reading tour in Europe, the apartment that he and Orlovsky were living in on E. 5th St. was condemned. Orlovsky found a cheap apartment here at 408 E. 10th St., where they lived in fourth-floor rooms from the summer of 1965 through March 1975. After that they moved a few blocks over to E. 12th St., which we'll pass later. While living on 10th St. Ginsberg began to achieve an international reputation. These were the years of his greatest political involvement. He worked passionately to end the Vietnam War, to fight censorship, and to liberalize drug laws. Much in demand for readings in America and abroad, he traveled extensively. His generosity to friends and poets was legendary. His political activism brought Abbie Hoffman, Jerry Rubin, Dave Dellinger, and Ed Sanders to the house, while Burroughs, Gregory Corso, Bob Dylan, Andrei Voznesensky, Lucien Carr, and many others often stayed with him here.

Many of Ginsberg's poems from this period were written in apartment 4C. One was about being mugged near the Peace Eye Book Store. Called "Mugging," it begins: "Tonite I walked out of my red apartment door on East Tenth street's dusk— / Walked out of my home ten years, walked out in my honking neighborhood . . ." He goes on to tell how a group of kids grabbed him, dragged him into a vacant cellar, and stole his wallet and a cheap watch, but ignored his poetry manuscripts worth thousands. (The neighborhood is somewhat safer today.)

Return to Avenue C, walk north to 12th St., and turn left one block to the corner of 12th and Avenue B.

17   Stanley's Bar

Stanley's Bar at 551 E. 12th St. on the northwest corner of Avenue B was owned by Stanley Tolkin, who later ran The Dom on St. Mark's Place. There's a bodega now in the old, five-story red brick building on this corner. Stanley Tolkin's bar, with cheap drinks and live piano music, was the center of the East Village underground community between 1962 and 1966. The Fugs' first performances were at Stanley's.

It was a relaxed and noncommercial place and had a slightly older clientele than the Annex down the street. Among its patrons: Ginsberg, David Henderson, Calvin Hernton, Tuli Kupferberg, Odetta, Ishmael Reed, Ed Sanders, and actors Lou Gossett, Moses Gunn, and Cicely Tyson. Walter Bowart tended bar here before moving on to publish the *East Village Other.*

Continue west on 12th St. past Avenue A and stop in front of the church on the left.

18   Allen Ginsberg and Peter Orlovsky/
Mary Help of Christians Church

Ginsberg and Orlovsky lived in a run-down, red brick tenement at 437 E. 12th St. for 21 years (1975-1996). Ginsberg described the apartment in many poems. Here's a quote from "In My Kitchen In New York": "The towels and pajama laundry's hanging on a rope in the hall . . . Turn right again — thru the door, God my office space, a mess of pictures & unanswered letters . . ." In a more recent poem, "The Charnel Ground," Ginsberg described a short walk from this apartment around the neighborhood— Christine's Restaurant, the Korean cleaners, the KK Polish Coffee Shop, and even the NYCE bank machine he used. This poem is its own guided tour.

Here as elsewhere, Ginsberg continued to host visitors, including the filmmaker Harry Smith, Gregory Corso, Philip Whalen, and hundreds of international poets and friends. When any acquaintance visited Manhattan, he provided a bed for them.

Directly across the street is the Mary Help of Christians Church at 438 E. 12th St., which figures in several of Ginsberg's poems. The ringing bells certainly would have been hard to escape, and Ginsberg incorporated them into several poems. In "Love Returned" he wrote, ". . . Well another day comes / Church bells have rung / dawn blue in New York . . ." In "Fourth Floor, Dawn, Up All Night Writing Letters" he begins, "Pigeons shake their wings on the copper church roof / out my window across the street, a bird perched on the cross / surveys the city's blue-gray clouds . . ."

Philip Whalen at Allen Ginsberg's apartment, 437 E. 12th St.
©Allen Ginsberg Trust. Courtesy of Fahey/Klein Gallery, Los Angeles.

Retrace your steps to Avenue A and turn right one block to the corner of Avenue A and 11th St.

19   Paradise Alley

Paradise Alley, ca. 1960s. Setting for Kerouac's
The Subterraneans.
Coutesy of Allen Ginsberg Archive, Stanford Univeristy

Unfortunately, the most important site in Kerouac's writings in the East Village, Paradise Alley, is now a vacant lot on the northeast corner of Avenue A and 11th St. A large brick building with an inner courtyard at 501 E. 11th St., it was torn down in the early 1980s. Here was the apartment of Alene Lee (Mardou Fox in *The Subterraneans*). Kerouac called the building "Heavenly Lane." The neighborhood still has vestiges of the old Italian district, but the gargoyles, frieze, and statue of Hera inside the courtyard are long gone. It was in the late summer of 1953 that Lee met Kerouac and Gregory Corso and had brief, turbulent affairs with both of them.

Kerouac saw the building as "something straight out of Dostoevski's Petersburg slums . . . the wash hung over the court, actually the back courtyard of a big 20-family tenement with bay windows, the wash hung out and in the afternoon the great symphony of Italian mothers, children, fathers BeFinneganing and yelling from stepladders, smells, cats mewing, Mexicans, the music from all the radios whether bolero of Mexican or Italian tenor of spaghetti eaters or loud suddenly turned-up KPFA symphonies of Vivaldi harpsichord intellectuals performances boom blam the tremendous sound of it which I then came to hear all the summer wrapt in the arms of my love—walking in there now, and going up the narrow musty stairs in a hovel, and her door." He has substituted the Berkeley, California radio station here because the entire action of *The Subterraneans* was transported in his fictional recounting to San Francisco, but all the events actually took place in New York City.

Ginsberg writes in "Howl": "...who ate fire in paint hotels and drank turpentine in Paradise Alley, death, or purgatoried their torsos night after night...", a reference, in Ginsberg's words, to "various artists lived in cheap hotels in the area, St. Mark's Place, their small rooms suffused with the smell of turpentine."

Walk west on 11th St. to the next corner, First Ave., and turn north for three blocks to 13th St. Along the way you'll pass the KK Coffee Shop and Christine's, mentioned in several of Ginsberg's poems. Turn left onto 13th to No. 338.

20   Joyce Glassman Johnson

In 1958 Joyce Glassman Johnson moved into apartment 3 at 338 E. 13th St. in the five-story beige and brown painted brick building between First and Second Avenues. She was escaping her parents' Upper West Side apartment. She wrote in *Minor Characters*, "my new apartment was small and had no light. Plants grew pale and died in the air-shaft window. The Pullman kitchen had been painted black by a previous occupant." Gregory Corso brought Kerouac to this apartment after he was beaten up outside the San Remo bar.

Return to First Ave. and walk one block north to 14th St. Look two blocks north to Beth Israel Hospital.

21   Beth Israel Hospital

In 1957, after Kerouac's head hit the curb outside the San Remo, Joyce Glassman took him to Beth Israel Hospital, at First Ave. and E. 16th St. Fearing he had suffered a concussion, Kerouac, already famous, didn't want to go, thinking he'd be recognized if they used his real name. So Joyce signed him in as Jack Glassman. She remembers him shouting "Cauterize my wounds!" at the emergency room door. The doctors washed and bandaged his head and found no sign of a concussion, but the event traumatized him so much

that some felt he was never quite the same afterward. (This is also the hospital in which Allen Ginsberg received the news in late March of 1997 that he had terminal liver cancer.)
Walk east on 14th St. to No. 404, above the McDonald's.

22   Allen Ginsberg

With the money Ginsberg received from the sale of his massive archive to Stanford University, he was able to buy a loft in this building in the fall of 1996. At 70 years of age he was beginning to find it difficult to climb the stairs in his old apartment, so he found this nearby elevator building, owned by Larry Rivers. Ginsberg had never owned a place in the city before and was quite happy furnishing the space with second-hand furniture from the Goodwill and Salvation Army stores that he loved. Ironically, on the very day that the last boxes of books were unpacked and placed on the shelves he discovered that he had liver cancer. He died in his bed here a week later on April 5, 1997, surrounded by family, friends, and old lovers. One of his last poems was written in this apartment, "Death and Fame."
Walk half a block west on the south side of 14th St. and stop at No. 324.

23   LeRoi and Hettie Jones

LeRoi and Hettie Cohen Jones lived in this old brick building at 324 E. 14th St. from February 1960 until 1962. Peter Orlovsky remembers helping them paint the apartment before they moved in. (At the time it had a stoop similar to the one still next door at No. 322.) They lived on the parlor floor above a dusty storefront occupied by Gypsies. The Gypsies were persistent in asking to tell Hettie Jones' fortune, but she never let them, recalling "I wanted to make up my own life." The Joneses had a sunny backyard filled with ailanthus trees that LeRoi called "poverty trees." LeRoi's first book, *Preface to a Twenty Volume Suicide Note*, was published in 1961 while he was living here. Several issues of their magazine, *Yugen*, were published here, too.

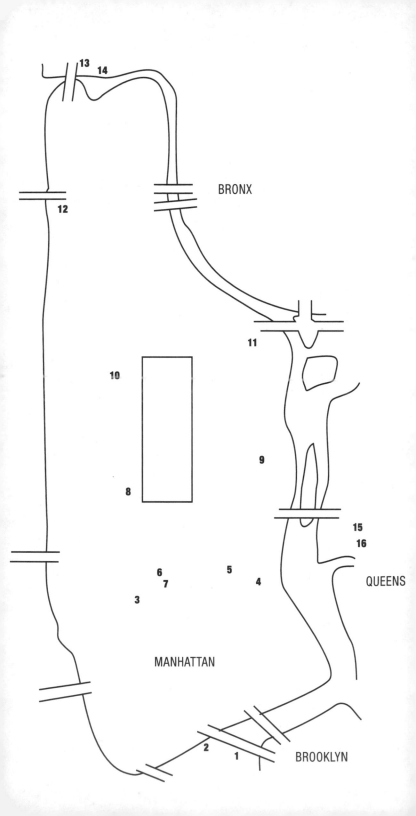

BRONX

10

8

9

11

15

16

6   5
7   4
3

QUEENS

MANHATTAN

12

13 14

2   1

BROOKLYN

Jack Kerouac at the Battery, Staten Island ferry dock, 1953.
©Allen Ginsberg Trust. Courtesy of Fahey/Klein Gallery, Los Angeles.

Far-flung Manhattan, Bronx, Queens, Yonkers

Other Beat Generation sites are outside the limits of these walking tours (which one hopes haven't proved too pedestrian!). But for rabid fans, here they are:

Manhattan

1 Brooklyn Bridge

Not only Hart Crane and Federico García Lorca, but Kerouac, Allen Ginsberg, and William Burroughs have all walked across the bridge and been inspired to write about it. In 1936 a fourteen-year-old Kerouac remembers walking over the Brooklyn Bridge in a snow storm. He was visiting his Grandma Ti Ma in Brooklyn and was enthralled by the sights of the big city. On this particular day, he passed his idol Thomas Wolfe walking across the bridge toward Manhattan. (Kerouac dreamt of living in New York City as he read Wolfe's novels.) Ferlinghetti wrote in an early poem that he "once started out to walk around the world, but that bridge was too much for me...."

The Brooklyn Bridge.
Photo by Bill Morgan.

2   Ambrose Lightship, South Street Seaport

Lawrence Ferlinghetti was stationed on the Ambrose Lightship when it was anchored outside of New York harbor during the winter of 1941-1942 in World War II. The Lightship is now on permanent exhibit at the foot of Fulton St.

3   Allen Ginsberg, 356 W. 27th St.

In late 1947 Allen Ginsberg rented an apartment in a building that once stood at 356 W. 27th St. He had returned to New York by way of Texas and Dakar, West Africa after a disappointing attempt at a love affair with Neal Cassady in Denver.

4   Bellevue Hospital, 1st Ave. at E. 28th St.

In 1939 William Burroughs was taken to the Bellevue psychiatric ward after cutting off his finger. Kerouac went to Bellevue's morgue to identify David Kammerer's body after it was pulled from the Hudson River following his demise. Joan Adams, Peter Orlovsky, and Michael Rumaker all visited the mental wards here.

5   John Clellon Holmes, 123 Lexington Ave.

In 1954-1955 John Clellon Holmes lived in an apartment in a brick row house at 123 Lexington Ave. between E. 28th and E. 29th. Kerouac visited frequently late at night.

6   New Yorker Hotel, 8th Ave. and W. 34th St.

Neal Cassady
©Allen Ginsberg Trust. Courtesy of Fahey/Klein Gallery Los Angeles.

In 1946, on his first trip to New York City, Neal Cassady worked in a parking lot next door to the New Yorker Hotel on 8th Ave. and W. 34th St.

7   Greyhound Bus Station, 242 W. 34th St.

When Kerouac, Ginsberg, or Neal Cassady took bus trips across the country they started, of course, from the Greyhound Bus Station that once stood at 242 W. 34th St. And so began the Road for many another young poet inspired by the Beats.

8   William Burroughs, 42 W. 60th St.

In 1945 William Burroughs inhabited a room above Riordan's Bar at 42 W. 60th St. Burroughs and Kerouac were sitting in this bar when they heard the news story about a fire in a zoo which ended with the phrase "and the hippos were boiled in their tank." They adopted this as the title of a collaborative story they were writing together. (The entire block of buildings has been demolished.)

9   Allen Ginsberg, 1401 York Ave., between 74th St. and 75th St.

From December 1, 1948 until the summer of 1949 Allen Ginsberg lived at 1401 York Ave. Herbert Huncke arrived at his door once completely worn out, feet bleeding, and seeming near death. Ginsberg wrote about this in "Howl": "... who walked all night with their shoes full of blood on the snowbank docks waiting for a door in the East River to open to a room full of steamheat and opium . . ." Ginsberg welcomed him and nursed him back to health, only to have Huncke begin storing stolen goods at the apartment as well as bringing two new thieves, Little Jack Melody and Vicki Russell, into the house. Melody was a petty criminal who burglarized cars and apartments with the help of Russell (a beautiful ex-hooker) and Huncke. Ginsberg felt helpless to stop them and was fascinated by their activities — although he never took part. Things came to a climax on April 21, 1949 when everyone loaded a car with the stolen merchandise to take it somewhere else. Ginsberg, heading to his brother's house, piled his own manuscripts into the car. With Jack Melody driving they set out. Melody panicked in Long Island City when a policeman tried to stop him for going down a one-way street the wrong way. When he tried to escape, his car crashed and turned over. Ginsberg made his way back to the apartment only to realize that his address was on the manuscripts left in the car. The police arrived shortly after and arrested everyone. The crime made the front page of the New York City tabloids. With the help of his father and a few of the Columbia professors, Ginsberg was sent to the nuthouse instead of to prison and there he met Carl Solomon. The building was replaced by a modern one long ago.

10   Allen Ginsberg, 200 W. 92nd St.

From October 1946 to July 1947, Allen Ginsberg lived in apartment 2W of the apartment building still standing at 200 W. 92nd St. He met Neal Cassady here, and dreamed up several of the poems later collected in *Empty Mirror*.

11   Allen Ginsberg, 321 E. 121st St.

This is where, during the summer of 1948, Allen Ginsberg had auditory visions of Blake speaking poetry in apartment 32, 321 E. 121st St. He wrote much here, echoing those visions. And they echoed in his poetry for the rest of his life.

12 New York State Psychiatric Institute of Columbia Presbyterian Hospital, 722 W. 168th St.

Allen Ginsberg met Carl Solomon, while being treated here between June 1949 and February 1950. The way they met is noted in Ginsberg's journal. "I'm Myshkin" [the saintly idiot of Dostoyevski], said Ginsberg. "I'm Kirilov" [the hard nihilist], said Solomon. At the age of 21, Solomon had admitted himself to the hospital where he asked for electro-shock therapy because he thought that he was mad. Ginsberg must have been having doubts about his own sanity at the time; his visions of Blake, his homosexuality (considered a mental illness in those days), and his involvement with the underworld of Herbert Huncke were all recent traumas.

Bronx and South Yonkers

13 Horace Mann High School, 231 W. 246th St., Northeast corner of Tibbett Ave.

Kerouac attended Horace Mann from 1939 to 1940 on a football scholarship. He lived with a relative in Brooklyn and made the two-hour commute daily via subway.

14 Lawrence Ferlinghetti, 106 Saratoga Ave.

Lawrence Ferlinghetti was born in a two-story wood house at 106 Saratoga Ave., a few hundred yards north of the northwest corner of Van Cortland Park. In a poem he records how he was born in a "small back bedroom" where his brother "heard the first cry."

Queens

15 Jack Kerouac, 133-01 Crossbay Blvd., Ozone Park

Kerouac's mother lived at 133-01 Crossbay Blvd. in the Ozone Park section of Queens from 1943 until 1948. In this building Kerouac wrote his first book, *The Town and the City*. It's the house where his father, Leo, died of cancer. A plaque commemorates Kerouac's passage through the ozone here.

16 Jack Kerouac, 94-21 134th St., Richmond Hill

After 1949, Kerouac's mother lived in an apartment at 94-21 134th St. in the Richmond Hill section. He wrote many books here, including *The Subterraneans, Maggie Cassidy,* and *Doctor Sax*. (Later he moved his mother to Florida, and thereby hangs his final tale.)

Who's Who

Adams, Joan Vollmer. Wife of William Burroughs, mother of William Burroughs, Jr., and a real friend to Kerouac, Allen Ginsberg, and other Beats around Morningside Heights in the early 1940s. It was in her apartment that most of the Columbia group first met. Portrayed as Jane in *The Subterraneans* and *On the Road*, and as Mary Dennison in *The Town and the City*. Accidentally killed by William Burroughs in Mexico City in 1952.

Amram, David. Versatile musician and eclectic composer. Performed poetry and jazz readings with Kerouac in the 1950s as well as the score of the film, *Pull My Daisy*.

Ansen, Alan. Poet and friend of Allen Ginsberg, William Burroughs, William Gaddis, and other Beats. Portrayed as Austin Bromberg in *The Subterraneans* and Rollo Greb in *On the Road*. Early secretary of W.H. Auden, he has lived in Greece for decades. Hosted the Beats in Tangier and Venice.

Ashbery, John. Poet-laureate of the New York School.

Baraka, Amiri. (see Jones, LeRoi)

Beck, Julian. Poet and co-founder with Judith Malina of The Living Theatre, one of the world's most revolutionary theater troupes. Produced ground-breaking plays such as *The Connection* and *The Brig*, as well as French avant-garde and Greek dramatists.

Berrigan, Ted. Poet closely associated with the St. Mark's Poetry Project. He conducted one of the most perceptive interviews with Kerouac.

Blackburn, Paul. Vermont poet who spent much of his career in lower New York, and co-edited *The Black Mountain Review*.

Black Mountain College. Important school for avant-garde art and literature in the mountains of North Carolina. Faculty included Charles Olson, Robert Creeley, and Robert Duncan. Closed in 1956.

Bremser, Ray. Poet, self-educated in the prison systems of New Jersey. Author of *Poems of Madness* and *Angel*.

Brossard, Chandler. Subterranean character who wrote the classic novel of 1940s hip life, *Who Walk in Darkness*.

Bruce, Lenny. Frequently arrested comedian who pushed the limits of censorship during the 1960s and often leapt over them.

Burroughs, William S. Novelist, author of *Junky, Naked Lunch,* and dozens of other Beat classics. Called Will Dennison in *The Town and the City* and Old Bull Lee in *On the Road*. Also known as "El Hombre Invisible."

Cannastra, William. Subterranean friend of Lucien Carr, Allen Ginsberg, and Kerouac. He became the subject of books by Kerouac and John Clellon Holmes; portrayed as Finistra in *Visions of Cody*. Died in a freak accident on the subway.

Carr, Lucien. One of the original group of friends at Columbia. He killed David Kammerer in Riverside Park. Portrayed as Kenny Wood in *The Town and the City* and Damion in *On the Road*. Went on to become the Washington Bureau Chief of UPI. "Howl" was originally dedicated to Carr, William Burroughs, Kerouac, and Neal Cassady, but Carr objected, and his name was dropped.

Cassady, Carolyn. Writer, artist, and wife of Neal Cassady and intimate friend of Kerouac. Called Camille in *On the Road* and Evelyn in *Visions of Cody*. Now living in London.

Cassady, LuAnne. Neal Cassady's first wife and subject of several of Kerouac's books. Portrayed as Mary Lou in *On the Road*.

Cassady, Neal. Legendary Denver stud upon whom Kerouac's most famous character in *On the Road*, Dean Moriarity, is based as well as Cody Pomeray in five other books. His exploits also attracted Ginsberg, John Clellon Holmes, Ken Kesey, and Tom Wolfe, among others. He looked and moved like the young Paul Newman in *The Hustler*.

Chase, Hal. Columbia friend of Allen Ginsberg and Kerouac. Portrayed as Chad King in *On the Road*. Later lived in Bolinas, California.

Corso, Gregory. Poet, author of *Gasoline* and *The Vestal Lady on Brattle*. Called Yuri Gligoric in *The Subterraneans*. Considered the *enfant terrible* of the Beats.

Cowen, Elise. Writer, Barnard graduate, friend of Joyce Glassman Johnson, was in love with Allen Ginsberg in the 1950s. She later committed suicide.

Cru, Henri. Horace Mann classmate of Kerouac. Remained a close friend and was a character in many of his books including Remi Boncoeur in *On the Road* and Deni Bleu in *Lonesome Traveler*.

Denby, Edwin. Witty poet and dance critic.

di Prima, Diane. Poet, author of *This Kind of Bird Flies Backward, Memoirs of a Beatnik,* and *Revolutionary Letters.* Edited *The Floating Bear* with LeRoi Jones. Now lives in San Francisco.

Elliott, Helen. Sometime girlfriend of Lucien Carr and friend of Kerouac. Portrayed as Ruth Erickson in *Desolation Angels.*

Ferlinghetti, Lawrence. Poet, painter, publisher of City Lights Books, and author of *Pictures of the Gone World, A Coney Island of the Mind*, and the new *A Far Rockaway of the Heart.* Portrayed as Lorenzo Monsanto in *Big Sur* (a name taken from his mother's family).

Frank, Robert. Seminal photographer and director of *Pull My Daisy.*

Garver, William. Junky buddy of William Burroughs and Allen Ginsberg, he supported himself through various endeavors, none legal. Called Old Bull Gaines in *Desolation Angels.*

Ginsberg, Allen. Poet, author of *Howl and Other Poems, Kaddish,* and a major Beat figure who was most instrumental in the creation and recognition of the Beat Generation. Portrayed as Leon Levinsky in *The Town and the City* and Carlo Marx in *On the Road.* Died in 1997.

Giorno, John. Poet, cohort of Burroughs, organizer of the Nova Convention.

Giroux, Robert. Kerouac's editor for *The Town and the City.*

Glassman, Joyce. see Johnson, Joyce Glassman.

Gould, Stanley. Crony of Kerouac, Allen Ginsberg, and Carl Solomon. He was the model for Ross Wallenstein in *The Subterraneans.*

Hart, Howard. Ohio-born writer who was one of the first poets in New York City to perform with a jazz backup. Now lives in San Francisco.

Haverty, Joan. Kerouac's second wife and mother of Jan Kerouac. Portrayed as Laura in *On the Road*.

Holmes, John Clellon. Kerouac confidant, and author of *Go* (the first Beat novel), *The Horn*, and *Get Home Free*.

Hornick, Lita. Writer and founder of the Kulcher Foundation, supporting writers and artists.

Huncke, Herbert. Writer, author of *The Evening Sun Turned Crimson*, and subject of many books and poems by the Beats. Portrayed as Tom Saybrook in *On the Road*. He introduced the Beats to the underworld of the Times Square drug scene and never lived it down.

Joans, Ted. Genial poet, author of *Jazz Poems* and *The Hipsters*, whose images are jazz-based. Spent many years abroad in Paris and Africa. Now lives in Seattle, WA.

Johnson, Joyce Glassman. Writer, editor, author of *Minor Characters*, and girlfriend of Kerouac. Portrayed as Alyce Newman in *Desolation Angels*, she is now an important novelist in her own right.

Jones, Hettie Cohen. Writer and editor of the seminal journal, *Yugen*, along with former husband, LeRoi Jones. Author of *How I Became Hettie Jones*.

Jones, LeRoi. Marxist writer, poet, and author of *Preface to a Twenty Volume Suicide Note* and *Blues People*. He edited *Yugen* with Hettie Jones, and *The Floating Bear* with Diane di Prima.

Kammerer, David. Friend of William Burroughs from St. Louis, murdered in 1943. Portrayed as Waldo Meister in *The Town and the City*.

Kandel, Lenore. Writer, author of *The Love Book*. Called Ramona Swartz in *Big Sur*.

Kerouac, Edie. see Parker, Edie

Kerouac, Jack. Writer, author of *The Town and the City, On the Road, The Subterraneans, Visions of Cody,* and many more novels. Leading figure in the Beat Generation.

Kerouac, Jan. Jack Kerouac's daughter and novelist, author of *Baby Driver*. Died in 1996.

Krim, Seymour. Writer, author of *Views of a Nearsighted Cannoneer*, and editor of the influential anthology *The Beats*. Horace Mann classmate of Kerouac.

Kupferberg, Tuli. Poet, musician, and a founder of the rock group The Fugs. (They are still performing, most recently in Italy.)

Lamantia, Philip. Surrealist poet, author of *Destroyed Works, The Blood of the Air,* and the new *Bed of Sphinxes.* Seen as Francis Da Pavia in *The Dharma Bums.*

Landesman, Fran and Jay. Playwrights, co-authored *The Nervous Set,* and edited *Neurotica* magazine, a precursor of Beat writing. Portrayed as Jay Chapman in *Visions of Cody.*

Laughlin, James. Affluent founder and publisher of New Directions Books.

Leary, Timothy. Psychedelic guru and explorer of inner peace. Ever the pioneer, upon his death in 1996 his ashes were blasted into outer space.

Lee, Alene. Mardou Fox, Kerouac's passing girlfriend in *The Subterraneans,* is based on her.

Leslie, Alfred. Artist and producer, along with Robert Frank, of *Pull My Daisy,* which was filmed in his loft.

Livornese, Tom. Early friend of Kerouac and a character in several of his novels.

Mailer, Norman. Novelist, author of *The Naked and the Dead* and *The White Negro: Superficial Reflections on the Hipster,* and most recently *The Gospel According to the Son.*

Malina, Judith. Co-founder of The Living Theatre, still active in the theater in New York.

Mekas, Jonas. Filmmaker, archivist, and founder of the Anthology Film Archives.

Melody, Jack. Petty criminal and pal of Herbert Huncke.

Micheline, Jack. Poet, author of *River of Red Wine,* introduced by Jack Kerouac. Now lives in San Francisco.

Morris, William. Greenwich Village poet who was arrested for performing poetry in Washington Square Park.

New York School Poets. Gathered around the St. Mark's Poetry Project in the 1960s. Included John Ashbery, Kenneth Koch, Ron Padgett, Ted Berrigan, Anne Waldman, and others.

Newman, Jerry. Friend of Kerouac, producer and owner of Esoteric Records.

O'Hara, Frank. Versatile poet and art critic, author of *Lunch Poems* and *Meditations in an Emergency.*

Orlovsky, Lafcadio. Brother of Peter Orlovsky.

Orlovsky, Peter. Raw poet, longtime partner of Allen Ginsberg, and author of *Clean Asshole Poems and Smiling Vegetable Songs.* Portrayed as Simon Darlovsky in *Desolation Angels.*

Parker, Charlie ("Bird"). Jazz legend, died too early.

Parker, Edie. Jack Kerouac's first wife, she and Joan Adams shared the apartment where the early Beats met. Seen as Judie Smith in *The Town and the City* and Edna Palmer in *Vanity of Duluoz.*

Rexroth, Kenneth. Dissident San Francisco poet, anarchist, and critic. Author of *Assays, Natural Numbers,* and translator of *100 Poems from the Chinese,* among many other texts important to the Beat writers for whom he was a kind of *pater familias.*

Rivers, Larry. Important avant-garde painter of the New York School.

Romney, Hugh. Fun poet, aka "Wavy Gravy" in the 1960s.

Russell, Vicki. Prostitute and petty criminal, erstwhile friend of Huncke and Ginsberg. Portrayed as Vicki in *Visions of Cody.*

Sanders, Ed. Founder of The Fugs rock group, and an important poet today. Now editor of the *Woodstock Journal.*

Smith, Harry. Filmmaker, music anthologist, and artist.

Solomon, Carl. Author of *Mishaps, Perhaps* and *More Mishaps,* to whom Allen Ginsberg addressed his most famous poem, "Howl."

Temko, Allan. Architectural critic, friend of Allen Ginsberg and Kerouac. Portrayed as Roland Major in *On the Road.* For many years he was the architectural critic for the *San Francisco Chronicle.*

Vega, Janine Pommy. Poet, former girlfriend of Peter Orlovsky, and author of *Poems to Fernando* and *Tracking the Serpent: Journeys to Four Continents* (City Lights Books, 1997).

Waldman, Anne. Poet, author of *Fast Speaking Woman* and *Iovis,* and director of the St. Mark's Poetry Project and Naropa's Jack Kerouac School of Disembodied Poetics.

Weaver, Helen. Girlfriend of Kerouac and friend of many of the Beats. Called Ruth Heaper in *Desolation Angels.*

Weaver, Ken. One of the founding Fugs, Ed Sanders' funky sixties rock group.

Weber, Steve. Another of the original Fugs.

White, Ed. Denver friend of Cassady and Columbia friend of Kerouac. Portrayed as Tim Grey in *On the Road.*

Wilentz, Eli and Ted. Owners of the Eighth Street Bookshop and publishers of Corinth Books. True friends and supporters of poets.

Bibliography of Works Consulted

Berrigan, Ted. *So Going Around Cities*. Berkeley, CA: Blue Wind Press, 1980.

Biner, Pierre. *The Living Theatre*. New York: Horizon Press, 1972.

Broyard, Anatole. *Kafka Was the Rage*. New York: Carol Southern Books, 1993.

Challis, Chris. *Quest for Kerouac*. London: Faber and Faber, 1984.

Charters, Ann, ed. *The Beats: Literary Bohemians in Postwar America*. Detroit, MI: Gale, 1983.

Charters, Ann. *A Bibliography of Works by Jack Kerouac*. New York: Phoenix Bookshop, 1975.

Cherkovski, Neeli. *Ferlinghetti: A Biography*. Garden City, New York: Doubleday & Co., 1979.

De Loach, Allen, ed. *The East Side Scene: American Poetry, 1960-1965*. Garden City, New York: Doubleday, 1972.

di Prima, Diane. *Memoirs of a Beatnik*. San Francisco, CA: Last Gasp, 1988.

Edmiston, Susan and Cirino, Linda. *Literary New York: A History and Guide*. Boston, MA: Houghton Mifflin, 1976.

Gifford, Barry and Lee, Lawrence. *Jack's Book: An Oral Biography of Jack Kerouac*. New York: St. Martin's Press, 1978.

Ginsberg, Allen. *Collected Poems: 1947-1980*. New York: Harper & Row, 1984.

Ginsberg, Allen. *Cosmopolitan Greetings: Poems 1986-1992*. New York: HarperCollins, 1994.

Ginsberg, Allen. *Howl: Original Draft Facsimile*. New York: Harper & Row, 1986.

Ginsberg, Allen. *Journals Early Fifties Early Sixties*. New York: Grove Press, 1977.

Ginsberg, Allen. *Journals Mid-Fifties 1954-1958*. New York: HarperCollins, 1995.

Ginsberg, Allen. *White Shroud: Poems 1980-1985.* New York: Harper & Row, 1986.

Glickman, Toby and Gene. *The New York Red Pages: A Radical Tourist Guide.* New York: Praeger, 1984.

Gruen, John. *The New Bohemia.* New York: Grosset & Dunlap, 1966.

Heide, Robert and Gilman, John. *Greenwich Village: A Primo Guide to Shopping, Eating, and Making Merry in True Bohemia.* New York: St. Martin's Griffin, 1995.

Holmes, John Clellon. *Go.* New York: New American Library, 1952.

Holmes, John Clellon. *Representative Men.* Fayetteville, AR: University of Arkansas Press, 1988.

Huncke, Herbert. *Guilty of Everything.* New York: Paragon House, 1990.

Johnson, Joyce. *Minor Characters.* Boston, MA: Houghton Mifflin, 1983.

Jones, Hettie. *How I Became Hettie Jones.* New York: E.P. Dutton, 1990.

Kerouac, Jack. *Book of Blues.* New York: Penguin Books, 1995.

Kerouac, Jack. *Desolation Angels.* New York: Coward-McCann, 1965.

Kerouac, Jack. *Lonesome Traveler.* New York: McGraw-Hill, 1960.

Kerouac, Jack. *On the Road.* New York: Viking, 1957.

Kerouac, Jack. *Selected Letters: 1940-1956.* Edited by Ann Charters. New York: Viking, 1995.

Kerouac, Jack. *The Subterraneans.* New York: Grove Press, 1958.

Kerouac, Jack. *The Town and the City.* New York: Harcourt Brace and Co., 1950.

Kerouac, Jack. *Vanity of Duluoz.* New York: Coward-McCann, 1968.

Kerouac, Jack. *Visions of Cody.* New York: McGraw-Hill, 1973.

Knight, Arthur and Glee, eds. *The Beat Book.* California, PA: Unspeakable Visions of the Individual, 1974.

Knight, Arthur and Kit, eds. *Beat Angels.* California, PA: Unspeakable Visions of the Individual, 1982.

Knight, Arthur and Kit, eds. *The Beat Diary.* California, PA: Unspeakable Visions of the Individual, 1977.

Landesman, Jay. *Rebel Without Applause.* New York: Paragon House, 1990.

Little, Stuart W. *Off-Broadway: The Prophetic Theater.* New York: Coward-McCann & Geoghegan, 1972.

McDarrah, Fred W. *Greenwich Village.* New York: Corinth, 1963.

McDarrah, Fred W. and McDarrah, Patrick J. *The Greenwich Village Guide.* Chicago, IL: A Cappella Books, 1992.

McDarrah, Fred W. *Kerouac & Friends: A Beat Generation Album.* New York: William Morrow and Co., 1985.

McNally, Dennis. *Desolate Angel: Jack Kerouac, the Beat Generation, and America.* New York: Random House, 1979.

McNeill, Don. *Moving Through Here.* New York: Knopf, 1970.

Malina, Judith. *The Diaries of Judith Malina 1947-1957.* New York: Grove Press, 1984.

Marqusee, Mike and Harris, Bill, eds. *New York: An Anthology.* Boston, MA: Little, Brown and Co., 1985.

Miles, Barry. *Ginsberg: A Biography.* New York: Simon and Schuster, 1989.

Miller, Terry. *Greenwich Village And How It Got That Way.* New York: Crown, 1990.

Morgan, Bill and Rosenthal, Bob, eds. *Best Minds: A Tribute to Allen Ginsberg.* New York: Lospecchio Press, 1986.

Morgan, Ted. *Literary Outlaw.* New York: Henry Holt and Co., 1988.

Nicosia, Gerald. *Memory Babe.* New York: Grove Press, 1983.

Osborne, Charles. *W.H. Auden: The Life of a Poet.* New York: Harcourt Brace Jovanovich, 1979.

Petronius. *New York Unexpurgated.* New York: Matrix House, 1966.

Pinchbeck, Daniel. "Children of the Beats." *New York Times Magazine,* Nov. 5, 1995.

Plumb, Stephen W. *The Streets Where They Lived.* St. Paul, MN: Marlor Press, 1989.

Rinzler, Alan, ed. *The New York Spy.* New York: David White Company, 1967.

Sager, Jessica. *A Guide to Literary Sites in the Union Square Area.* New York: Teachers & Writers Collaborative, 1993.

Schumacher, Michael. *Dharma Lion: A Critical Biography of Allen Ginsberg.* New York: St. Martin's Press, 1992.

Silesky, Barry. *Ferlinghetti: the Artist in his Time.* New York: Warner Books, 1990.

Solomon, Carl. *Emergency Messages.* New York: Paragon House, 1989.

Stelter, Lawrence. *By the El: Third Avenue and its El at Mid-Century.* Flushing, New York: H&M Productions, 1995.

Sukenick, Ronald. *Down and In: Life in the Underground.* New York: Beech Tree Books/William Morrow, 1987.

Tytell, John. *Naked Angels: The Lives and Literature of the Beat Generation.* New York: McGraw-Hill, 1976.

Wakefield, Dan. *New York in the Fifties.* Boston, MA: Houghton Mifflin/Seymour Lawrence, 1992.

Waldman, Anne, ed. *Out of This World.* New York: Crown, 1991.

Wallock, Leonard, ed. *New York: Culture Capital of the World, 1940-1965.* New York: Rizzoli, 1988.

Watson, Steven. *The Birth of the Beat Generation.* New York: Pantheon Books, 1995.

Yeadon, David. *Nooks and Crannies: An Unusual Walking Tour Guide to New York City.* New York: Charles Scribner's Sons, 1979.

Index

Beat Titles from City Lights

William Burroughs
THE BURROUGHS FILE
YAGE LETTERS

Neal Cassady
THE FIRST THIRD

Gregory Corso
GASOLINE: Pocket Poets #8

Diane di Prima
PIECES OF A SONG: Selected Poems

Lawrence Ferlinghetti
PICTURES OF THE GONE WORLD: Pocket Poets #1
THE CITY LIGHTS POCKET POETS ANTHOLOGY
   (selections from the entire series, edited by Ferlinghetti)

Allen Ginsberg
THE FALL OF AMERICA: Pocket Poets #30
HOWL & OTHER POEMS: Pocket Poets #4
KADDISH & OTHER POEMS: Pocket Poets #14
MIND BREATHS: Pocket Poets #35
PLANET NEWS: Pocket Poets #23
PLUTONIAN ODE: Pocket Poets #40
REALITY SANDWICHES: Pockets Poets #18

Jack Kerouac
BOOK OF DREAMS
POMES ALL SIZES: Pocket Poets #48
SCATTERED POEMS: Pocket Poets #28
SCRIPTURE OF THE GOLDEN ETERNITY: Pocket Poets #51

Philip Lamantia
BED OF SPHINXES: Selected Poems

David Meltzer
SAN FRANCISCO BEAT: Talking with the Poets
   (interviews with 13 Bay Area Beat poets)

Also, two books of 20 detachable postcards:
POSTCARDS FROM THE UNDERGROUND: Portraits of the Beat Era
   by Larry Keenan
TRAVELS WITH GINSBERG: A Postcard Book
   Allen Ginsberg photographs, 1944–1997